Praise for *Discover the Royal You!*

Victoria has a contagious passion for the Kingdom of God. Her Bible study series and bi-annual women's conferences have been the central discipleship tools for the spiritual growth of the women of our church. She has led the women as they gather around the Word of God. This Bible study series is rich with the fragrance of the presence of God.

Each year we have seen remarkable spiritual growth and thriving relationships within the women who participate in her Bible studies. This is due to Victoria's ability to present the Bible in a deeply spiritual, and yet simply practical way. She has allowed the Word of God to form her life and this Bible study series is the result of that personal, intimate spiritual formation. I am excited for her Bible study series to spread across the nation, producing the same fruit that we have seen within our congregation.

> Evan Martin, M.Div.
> Pastor
> Colorado Church
> Glendale, Colorado

✑

Too often, young girls are the earliest victims of "identify theft." Mercilessly stolen by Satan in childhood, their female identities are defined by others, and reinforced through the twisted perception of the world. Victoria Munro's *Discover the Royal You!* Bible study lovingly and confidently, guides women into deeper understanding of God's unfathomable love, identity, and purpose for them. Victoria's heart for women is profoundly rooted in essential spiritual truths leading women to identify and appreciate themselves as the Father does; to walk in His promises for them and reign as His royal daughters! This is the ultimate freedom for girls and women of all ages.

> Debra W. Hudson, Ph.D.
> Dean of Social Sciences and Humanities
> Colorado Christian University
> Founder of *Walk on Water: Ministry to Women*

Our true identity and the love of the Father were two of the hardest things for me to grasp when I first set foot into the Bethel School of Supernatural Ministry in Redding, California. Who did God make me to be and why? How could He really love me that much? I was not alone. This was a struggle for many, and until we truly "got it" at a heart and spirit level, the leaders would not let us move on to all they had to teach us.

This world needs hope. That hope can only be found when we realize the power, purpose, and authority God bestows on His sons and daughters to make a difference in our world. We are not paupers, we are princesses and princes in the Kingdom of the Creator of the Universe. And we are not alone. Our loving Father, Jesus, and the Holy Spirit are with us every moment and every step. My close friend, Victoria Munro, has walked this walk and she lovingly and compassionately has put herself and her heart into every part of this study as she allows Holy Spirit, through her writing, to lead us into the freedom and destiny of the supernatural life with God. I highly endorse this study. We can listen to our mentors' online sermons, and sit in the pews on Sunday, and read all the great authors...but until we dig into the Word of God for ourselves, we will not reach that intimate place where our Papa can transform our lives.

> Chris Tracy, Denver, Colorado
> Author - *Tapestry - The Divine Design for Your Life*
> Founder - Beautiful Smart Lady Summit
> www.breadwineministries.com

❧

Imagine doing a Bible study that touches the deep places in your heart and makes the Word of God come alive! Victoria has a gift to write Bible studies which heal hurting hearts, cause readers to see themselves as God sees them, and rest in His incredible promises. It makes such a difference in life when you know and really believe you are chosen, hand-picked by a good and gracious Father God.

Discover the Royal You! draws and encourages you to search and experience deep, yet very practical truths from God's Word. You will learn to recognize and eliminate debilitating lies from the enemy, and enjoy living fully in your royal calling. This study will prompt you to appropriately use the authority the Lord Jesus died and rose again to give us. You will not only see yourself as who you truly are—a co-heir with the King of kings, but you will complete this study motivated and filled with hope to pursue your divine destiny!

Nancy Paul
Biblical Counselor
Jubilee Fellowship Church

❧

Because so many Christians live in the "fast lane" of life, believers need help slowing down. When their pace is readjusted to the speed their creator designed them to move, they can take stock of where they are spiritually. The flow of the Good News from sermons, seminars, books and the airways commonly become a list of good intentions, but somehow never take root into practical application and fruition.

If you are seeking a place and a way to bring fruition and momentum to your good intentions and higher spiritual pursuits, you are going to find that Victoria's *Discover the Royal You!: Training for Reigning*, is that practical path to take you higher. Victoria's track record of overcoming, her passion and illumination of God's Word is contagious!
Get prepared to be trained. Get prepared to be grounded. Get prepared to be changed and used by God!

Jackie Jacobsen
Led by the Spirit School
Teacher and Founder

❧

I have used the *Discover the Royal You! Training for Reigning* Bible study series to encourage women in my neighborhood to draw closer to the Lord and each other by studying God's Word together. It has been such a blessing to watch the love and fellowship grow between the neighbor gals. There is power in the Word of God: It brings salvation and healing to the heart.

As we have grown closer to our heavenly Father through *Discover the Royal You!* lessons, we have all grown so much closer to each other. Comforting and praying for one another has truly blessed our neighborhood community. *Training for Reigning* has inspired us to be the hands and feet of feet of Jesus to each other.

Thank you for this wonderful study!

Shari Underwood

⌇

Victoria's studies masterfully pull together verses from the Word of God to illuminate and illustrate the wonderful truths about our Lord. Her insightful questions encourage the heart to ponder, engage, interact and dialog with our Savior. She has wonderfully captured the art of combining the study of God's Word and the opening of the heart to commune with God.

Karen Ross
Home Smart Realty Group

⌇

I have gone through several of Victoria's *Honey for Your Soul* Bible Studies. *Discover the Royal You! Training for Reigning* is a fundamental and foundational study that reaches to new Christians as well as seasoned ones. It truly has Godly revelations laced throughout that everyone can relate to. This study guides you through the critical points in every believer's life and encourages their spiritual level of growth. She encourages you to constantly seek the Holy Spirit to reveal the truths of God and to uncover the lies of the enemy that are keeping you from every good thing God has for you. I am more confident now to walk in the true royal identity God intended for me, and I believe you will be too!

Alison McCoy

⌇

I have so many great things to say about the *Discover the Royal You!* Bible study. I really believe that if you follow it with the heart to get closer to God, you cannot help but to do that, and in the process fall even more in love with Him. It is heavily structured in the Word and brings with it a catalyst for growth, freedom and the redemptive promises that help to shed light on the identity that God desperately desires his royal children to find.

    Melita Quinonez

❧

This study was soul searching, insightful, and empowering as I examined the Biblical truths of my royal identity. I was able to identify those hidden encumbrances to truly owning that I am a daughter of the King. How freeing to feel I can walk in the love, power, and authority that God has for me!

    Suzanne Simpson
    Licensed Counselor with Renewed Life Counseling

Discussion Group Leaders' Guide

for

Discover the Royal You!

Training for Reigning

Victoria Munro

Honey for your Soul

Bible Study Series

Cover Design by Victoria Munro
Interior Layout by Nick Zelinger, NZ Graphics

Books may be purchased for sales promotion
By contacting the publisher

Honey for Your Soul, LLC
303-345-3201 • www.HoneyForYourSoul.com

ISBN: 978-0-9777872-1-0 (print edition)

First Edition

Printed in the United States of America

❦

This Bible study series is dedicated to Judy Leonard, Pat Lawler
and to the many other devoted and godly teachers who have helped
to shape my life and point me to Christ. The incredible love and patience
they demonstrated as well as their life-giving words will never be forgotten.

❦

Contents

Before You Get Started

You are worthy to take the scroll
and break its seals and open it.
For you were slaughtered, and your blood has ransomed people for God
from every tribe and language and people and nation.
¹⁰And you have caused them to become
a Kingdom of priests for our God.
And they will reign on the earth.
Revelation 5:9-10

Discover the Real, Royal You!

In order to discover and embrace our royal identity in Christ, we need first to recognize and believe the truth that God is always utterly, completely good; that He loves us deeply and desires the very best for us. Only then can we see ourselves as we really are—as He sees us— royal sons and daughters of the King!

For this reason, we begin this study series by focusing on God's goodness, His great love for us and the fact that He earnestly desires relationship with us. I pray that as you study this series the Holy Spirit will open your heart and mind to new dimensions of how totally good your heavenly Father is and how passionately and extravagantly He loves you. May He reveal to you in new ways and at increasingly deeper levels who you really are—who He's created you to be and what He's equipped and destined you to become and do on this earth and for eternity.

Seeing ourselves as we really are—as God sees us—isn't always easy. At times it seems as though our past, the world around us, and sometimes negative voices inside our own heads are determined to distort God's view of who we really are.

We can easily allow others to influence how we view ourselves. Even though it might have been years ago, what our parents or other significant people said to or about us in our early years often affects how we see ourselves today. We may also let our performance define us—how we measure up, or fail to measure up, to the expectations of others or even our own expectations.

> "Jesus came to announce to us that an identity based on success, popularity and power is a false identity—an illusion! Loudly and clearly he says: 'You are not what the world makes you; but you are children of God.'"
>
> ~ Henri J. M. Nouwen, *Here and Now: Living in the Spirit*

Both hourly and daily, we are surrounded by negative messages, through ads, "self-help" articles and books, video clips and other assorted media, that degrade our self-concept. We don't even notice it anymore because we have internalized and integrated the message that we're not valuable as we are.

The average person is exposed to between three and five thousand advertising messages every day! These messages are carefully crafted to make us feel unlovable and unworthy unless we buy whatever they're selling. And we're threatened with ruin unless we wear a certain kind of clothing or drive a particular car etc.

Consciously, we know this isn't true, practical or possible. Yet these messages affect viewers and listeners in deep and profound ways. As a result, low self-esteem, insecurity, depression and even self-hatred are widespread, even among Christians. The only antidote is to see ourselves as God sees us—the One who created us, chose us and loves us passionately.

> "Sociologists have a theory of the looking-glass self: you become what the most important person in your life (wife, father, boss, etc.) thinks you are. How would my life change if I truly believed the Bible's astounding words about God's love for me, if I looked in the mirror and saw what God sees?"
>
> ~ Philip Yancey, *What's So Amazing About Grace?*

This study series is designed to not only counteract the subtle but powerful lies we're exposed to daily, but also to equip us to recognize, believe, and live as the royal children of the King we truly are. God desires that we trust Him, learn to see ourselves as He sees us, and then freely pursue our divine destiny here on earth and forever.

❧

Why Use the Bible as Our Source?

> *Then my father taught me, saying:*
> *"Never forget my words;*
> *If you do everything I teach you,*
> *You'll reign in life!"*
> Proverbs 4:4 (TPT)

The Bible is no ordinary book. It's been described as God's love letter—a personal message from Almighty God himself addressed to you! Its words are like food and medicine to nourish and heal your soul. Only God's Word will reveal the truth about who you really are. The words in this book are alive and powerful—truths that *will* change your life. As you study the Bible, you'll increasingly see God, yourself and the world around you from His viewpoint.

> *Dear friend, listen well to my words;*
> *tune your ears to my voice.*
> *Keep my message in plain view at all times.*
> *Concentrate! Learn it by heart!*
> *Those who discover these words live, really live;*
> *body and soul, they're bursting with health.*
> Proverbs 4:20-22 (MSG)

As the writer of Proverbs says, 'God's words are life!' The Holy Spirit reveals truth to us as we read and study God's Word. When we go through difficult times, His Word comforts, guides, strengthens and encourages us. If we know the Scriptures and His promises, we can pray and/or speak these powerful words into the situations we encounter.

*For the word of God is alive and powerful. It is sharper than
the sharpest two-edged sword, cutting between soul and spirit,
between joint and marrow. It exposes our innermost thoughts
and desires.*
Hebrews 4:12

Studying the Bible also builds our faith. As we understand more about the person and character of God from his Word, we're better able to trust him. We can count on a God we know; One who is always entirely good, loves us deeply and has only good plans for us. He's the only One worthy of our trust.

~

My Own Experience

For almost fifty years, I've regularly studied the Bible and it has completely changed my life. I'm very grateful to God for this, but it didn't happen overnight and it wasn't automatic. I encourage you, if you want to know God more intimately and become more like His Son, take time to regularly study the Bible.

Knowing God's Word has proved invaluable—it's been truly lifesaving to me in tough times. I doubt I would have survived without it. If you take time to study the Bible with an open heart to the Holy Spirit, you will be changed. And it *doesn't* have to take you fifty years!

However, we will grow in our knowledge of God and understanding of his Word in direct proportion to the amount of time and energy we're willing to invest. Driving in Colorado's mountain canyons, I sometimes see people panning for gold in the rivers. They're really dedicated—standing for hours often in freezing water, hoping to find a nugget of gold. I've often wondered what amazing things God would have done in, for and through them if they'd spent that time studying His Word. It reminds me of the challenge made by the writer of Proverbs:

*My child, listen to what I say,
and treasure my commands.*

> [2] *Tune your ears to wisdom,*
>   *and concentrate on understanding.*
> [3] *Cry out for insight,*
>   *and ask for understanding.*
> [4] *Search for them as you would for silver;*
>   *seek them like hidden treasures.*
> [5] *Then you will understand what it means to fear the LORD,*
>   *and you will gain knowledge of God.*
> [6] *For the LORD grants wisdom!*
>   *From his mouth come knowledge and understanding.*
> Proverbs 2:1-6

Benefits of Studying the Bible This Way

As we grow in Christ, it's important we learn to study God's Word for ourselves and not depend only on the teaching of others, beneficial as that is. Consider this challenge from the writer of Hebrews:

> *You have been believers so long now that you ought to be teaching others. Instead, you need someone to teach you again the basic things about God's word. You are like babies who need milk and cannot eat solid food.* [13] *For someone who lives on milk is still an infant and doesn't know how to do what is right.* [14] *Solid food is for those who are mature, who through training have the skill to recognize the difference between right and wrong.* Hebrews 5:12-14

One of the best ways to be prepared for and benefit from this "solid food" state is through Bible study.

There are many excellent ways to study the Bible and I've found the method we use in this study series to be helpful and effective. These studies are designed to guide you through a specific topic or book of the Bible and help you develop a deeper understanding of its spiritual truths. Our goal isn't simply to provide you with more information, though of course that's valuable. Our aim is to challenge you to question and think more deeply about what you're studying. Also to give you opportunity to hear from God and respond personally to what you're learning in a way that will impact your everyday life. Growing in this way will make you more like Jesus!

Many of the scriptures referenced in these studies have been printed in full for you. However I strongly encourage you to look up and prayerfully read those that are especially meaningful to you in different translations.

c/つ

Suggested Study Guidelines:

Purposely set time aside to study. Find a time that works well for you and make an appointment with God.

Find a place you enjoy. Ideally this would be a quiet room in your home where you can be alone, feel comfortable and connect with God without having to deal with interruptions.

Keep your study materials close by. Of course, your Bible, a pen and notebook, tablet or computer are necessary to your study. It would also be helpful to have several different translations, a Bible dictionary and a concordance, if they are available to you.

Prepare your heart. Talk to God and ask Him to reveal and remove anything that may block you from receiving revelation during your study. You may sense you need to repent for something you've done or said, or perhaps you need to forgive someone.

Ask the Holy Spirit to guide you. Jesus promised the Holy Spirit would give us understanding and reveal more of Jesus to us—which He loves to do! He inspired the Word of God, so invite Him to bring clarity and reveal new facets of the topic you're studying. Ask Him to show you what changes He'd like to see in your life in light of what you're learning. (John 16:13-14)

Meditation is an important part of your study. To meditate means to think deeply and continuously, ponder, contemplate or reflect. It also means to murmur, to mutter and to converse with oneself. Preparing your study ahead of time gives you opportunity to meditate on it and gain further insights to share in your small discussion group.

Look at the 'big picture' first. Read through the passages you're studying in order to see them in context. Do this several times, if possible using different translations.

Be a doer of the Word. We conclude each study with one or two application questions. These are really important, so allow enough time to answer them prayerfully. (Matthew 7:24-27)

> *But don't just listen to God's word. You must do what it says.*
> *Otherwise, you are only fooling yourselves.*
> James 1:22

Be ready to share what you've learned in your small group. In this way you'll learn from one another what the Holy Spirit has revealed to each of you. It also gives a venue to discuss questions you have and/or verses and concepts that weren't clear to you. You'll also have opportunity to pray for and minister to one another.

As you study the Bible in this way, there is no limit to the wealth of truth, understanding and growth that will result!

> "The Bible is the inevitable outcome of God's continuous speech.
> It is the infallible declaration of His mind." ~ A.W. Tozer

❧

Declarations—Our Words Are Powerful

> *Words kill, words give life;*
> *they're either poison or fruit—you choose.*
> Proverbs 18:21 (MSG)

Since God spoke everything into existence, and we're created in His image, our words carry creative power. God's truth is reinforced in our lives when we declare—even prophesy—it over ourselves. Even if what we're declaring may not seem true at the time or isn't currently a part of our lives, by making declarations we're speaking God's life into situations. This doesn't mean we're lying or denying the truth, but rather focusing on and declaring the greater truth of God's Word.

Hearing the declarations we make out loud over ourselves will change us. It will change the way we think, how we view God, and the way we see ourselves and our circumstances. Romans 10:17 highlights this, *So then faith comes by hearing, and hearing by the word of God.* Because of this we've included relevant declarations at the beginning of each study. Try speaking these aloud each day while you're studying that section and see what happens.

Quotation Authors

Throughout these studies, I have included quotations from other authors. I've done this to reinforce or emphasize a truth from someone else's perspective. Because the men and women quoted have various backgrounds, come from different places and times in history, what they wrote also adds fresh insight and inspiration. I've included a very brief bio on each of those quoted in Endnotes after Study Six.

My Prayer for You

My heart's desire and prayer for you as you study this series is that you will experience in a deeper way than ever before how extravagantly your heavenly Father loves you. I'm asking God that you'll see yourself increasingly as He sees you—a royal prince or princess, and that you'll become increasingly confident in your royal role. I know God wants this for you too!

Often, our understanding of ourselves—who we are—has become self-defined rather than God-defined. I trust that through this study series you'll understand, believe and increasingly enjoy living in all that Christ says you are. It is a journey; a process.

As you study *Discover the Royal You!*, may you recognize your true identity and see yourself increasingly as His masterpiece, which you truly are. I pray you will also learn to exercise your God-given authority and fully live as a royal child of the King!

> *For we are God's masterpiece. He has created us anew in Christ Jesus,*
> *so we can do the good things he planned for us long ago.*
> Ephesians 2:10

❦

"A Christian is not simply a person who is forgiven and goes to heaven. A Christian, in terms of his or her deepest identity, is a saint, a spiritually born child of God, a divine masterpiece, a child of light, a citizen of heaven." ~ Neil T. Anderson

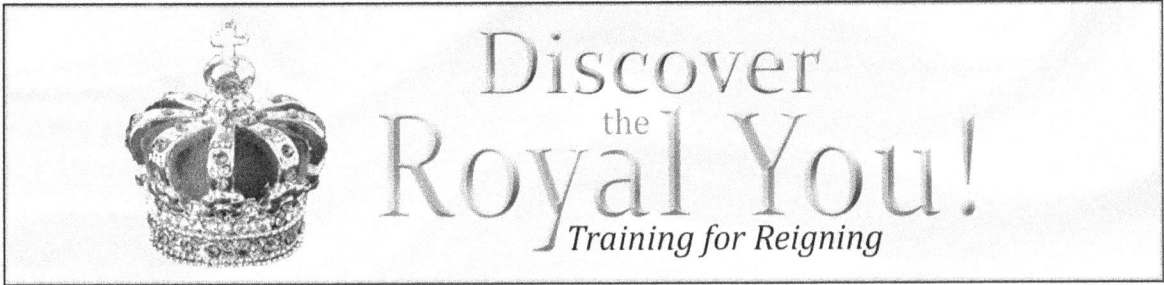

Study One
The Goodness of God

A. Reflect on the Goodness of God

To truly understand who we are in Christ and enjoy His love, we must know and trust Him. We need to know Him both experientially and personally, not simply know about Him intellectually. When we fully believe that He is utterly good, all powerful, loves us unconditionally, and has our best interests at heart, it's a lot easier to trust Him.

> "The original Saxon meaning of our English word 'God' is 'The Good.' God is not only the Greatest of all beings, but the best. All the goodness there is in any creature has been imparted from the Creator, but God's goodness is underived, for it is the essence of His eternal nature." ~ A.W. Pink

Declarations:

- God is utterly good all the time. (Psalm 119:68)

- God's wrath and judgment were poured out on Christ at the cross so that His goodness can be poured out on and through me. (Romans 3:23-26)

- You are a good God! I eagerly look forward to experiencing Your goodness today! (Psalm 31:19)

1. Before looking at the Scriptures, write down what comes to mind when you think about the goodness of God.

2. What can you learn about the goodness of God from the following passages?

The LORD replied, "I will make all my goodness pass before you, and I will call out my name, Yahweh, before you. For I will show mercy to anyone I choose, and I will show compassion to anyone I choose.
Exodus 33:19

Yet I am confident I will see the LORD's goodness
* while I am here in the land of the living.*
Psalm 27:13

You are good and do only good;
* teach me your decrees.*
Psalm 119:68

This is the message we heard from Jesus and now declare to you: God is light, and there is no
darkness in him at all.
1 John 1:5

3. Meditate on Psalm 34:8. What are some practical ways you can "taste and see that the Lord is good"?

Taste and see that the LORD is good.
  Oh, the joys of those who take refuge in him!
Psalm 34:8

4. King David experienced and appreciated God's goodness. What aspects of His goodness does he describe in Psalm 23?

    A psalm of David
    The LORD is my shepherd;
      I have all that I need.
    ² He lets me rest in green meadows;
      he leads me beside peaceful streams.
    ³   He renews my strength.
    He guides me along right paths,
      bringing honor to his name.
    ⁴ Even when I walk
      through the darkest valley,
    I will not be afraid,
      for you are close beside me.

Your rod and your staff
   protect and comfort me.
[5] *You prepare a feast for me*
   in the presence of my enemies.
You honor me by anointing my head with oil.
   My cup overflows with blessings.
[6] *Surely your goodness and unfailing love will pursue me*
   all the days of my life,
and I will live in the house of the LORD
   forever.

5. For which aspects of God's goodness are you especially grateful?

"Expecting to taste and see His goodness keeps us impervious to the mental and emotional breakdowns that violate who He designed us to be—carriers of hope, and models of His goodness." ~ Bill Johnson, *God Is Good: He's Better than You Think*

∞

Everything God Does Is Good

6.   How do the following passages reveal God's goodness through His actions?

⁴ And God saw that the light was good. Then he separated the light from the darkness.
¹⁰ God called the dry ground 'land' and the waters "seas." And God saw that it was good.
¹⁸ to govern the day and night, and to separate the light from the darkness. And God saw that it was good.
Genesis 1:4, 10, 18

Thank you for making me so wonderfully complex!
*   Your workmanship is marvelous—how well I know it.*
Psalm 139:14

7. What do the following verses tell about God's goodness to all?

How great is the goodness
    you have stored up for those who fear you.
You lavish it on those who come to you for protection,
  blessing them before the watching world.
Psalm 31:19

He loves whatever is just and good;
    the unfailing love of the LORD fills the earth.
Psalm 33:5

O Lord, you are so good, so ready to forgive,
so full of unfailing love for all who ask for your help.
Psalm 86:5

The LORD helps the fallen
and lifts those bent beneath their loads.
[15] *The eyes of all look to you in hope;*
you give them their food as they need it.
[16] *When you open your hand,*
you satisfy the hunger and thirst of every living thing.
[17] *The LORD is righteous in everything he does;*
he is filled with kindness.
Psalm 145:14-17

8. From Romans 2:4, explain how awareness of God's goodness brings about repentance in a way that difficulties or fear of punishment cannot.

Don't you see how wonderfully kind, tolerant, and patient God is with you? Does this mean nothing to you? Can't you see that his kindness is intended to turn you from your sin?
Romans 2:4

"The goodness of God is seen in the variety of natural pleasures which He has provided for His creatures. God might have been pleased to satisfy our hunger without the food being pleasing to our palates—how His benevolence appears in the varied flavors which He has given to meats, vegetables, and fruits! God has not only given us senses, but also that which gratifies them; and this too reveals His goodness. The earth might have been as fertile as it is without its surface being so delightfully variegated. Our physical lives could have been sustained without beautiful flowers to regale our eyes, and exhale sweet perfumes. We might have walked the fields without our ears being saluted by the music of the birds. Whence, then, this loveliness, this charm, so freely diffused over the face of nature? Verily, 'The tender mercies of the Lord are over all His works' (Psalm 145:9)." ~ A. W. Pink

9.   What does God promise in Psalm 84:11

For the LORD God is our sun and our shield.
   He gives us grace and glory.
The LORD will withhold no good thing
   from those who do what is right.
Psalm 84:11

10. What is one area in your life or your circumstances where you're aware that you're not acting in a way that demonstrates your trust in God's goodness?

B. God's Goodness Revealed in Jesus

'Is he – quite safe? I shall feel rather nervous about meeting a lion.' 'Safe?' said Mr. Beaver. 'Who said anything about safe? 'Course he isn't safe! But he's good. He's the king, I tell you.'" ~ C.S. Lewis, *The Chronicles of Narnia*

11. What can you glean about Jesus' goodness as God from Matthew 19:16-17?

Someone came to Jesus with this question: "Teacher, what good deed must I do to have eternal life?"
[17] *"Why ask me about what is good?"Jesus replied. "There is only One who is good. But to answer your question—if you want to receive eternal life, keep the commandments."*
Matthew 19:16-17

12. What aspects of God's goodness does Jesus express in the following verse?

So don't be afraid, little flock. For it gives your Father great happiness to give you the Kingdom.
Luke 12:32

13. How is the goodness of God revealed in Jesus' action in the following passages?

But now God has shown us a way to be made right with him without keeping the requirements of the law, as was promised in the writings of Moses and the prophets long ago. 22 We are made right with God by placing our faith in Jesus Christ. And this is true for everyone who believes, no matter who we are.

23For everyone has sinned; we all fall short of God's glorious standard. 24Yet God freely and graciously declares that we are righteous. He did this through Christ Jesus when he freed us from the penalty for our sins. 25 For God presented Jesus as the sacrifice for sin. People are made right with God when they believe that Jesus sacrificed his life, shedding his blood. This sacrifice shows that God was being fair when he held back and did not punish those who sinned in times past, 26 for he was looking ahead and including them in what he would do in this present time. God did this to demonstrate his righteousness, for he himself is fair and just, and he declares sinners to be right in his sight when they believe in Jesus.
Romans 3:21-26

And you know that God anointed Jesus of Nazareth with the Holy Spirit and with power. Then Jesus went around doing good and healing all who were oppressed by the devil, for God was with him.
Acts 10:38

Our Response to God's Goodness

"The more we know God's goodness, the more we trust Him. The more we trust Him, the easier it is for us to put our lives into His hands. Only by placing our lives in His hands can we open the way for Him to save us, bless us and work through us, so that His wonderful will can be done on earth as it is done in heaven."
~ Gloria Copeland

14. How does God want us to respond to His goodness?

I will sing to the LORD
  because he is good to me.
Psalm 13:6

Praise the LORD, for the LORD is good;
  celebrate his lovely name with music.
Psalm 135:3

Give thanks to the Lord, for he is good!
  His faithful love endures forever.
Psalm 136:1

The LORD is good,
  a strong refuge when trouble comes.
  He is close to those who trust in him.
Nahum 1:7

15. From this study, which aspects of God's goodness were especially meaningful to you?

16. In light of this, how can you cooperate with God to enjoy and live in the truth of His goodness?

"The highest good, than which there is no higher, is God, and consequently He is unchangeably good, hence truly eternal and truly immortal. All other good things are only from Him." ~ Augustine of Hippo

For a more in-depth study on the Goodness of God, see Honey for Your Soul's *In His Eyes, Studies on the Character of God, Study Three – The Goodness of God.*

In the next study, you'll delve more deeply into what it means to be chosen, deeply loved and adopted into the family of an absolutely good God and Father!

"To be loved by God is the highest relationship, the highest achievement, and the highest position in life." ~ Henry Blackaby

Prayer Requests and Notes

Study Two
Loved, Chosen and Adopted

A. Loved by God

"'God is love' (1 John 4:8). It is not simply that God 'loves,' but that He is Love itself. Love is not merely one of His attributes, but His very nature." ~ A.W. Pink

Declarations:

- God loves me in the same way He loves His Son Jesus. (John 15:9)

- God's love for me never changes—no matter how I feel, what I do or fail to do. (Hebrews 13:8)

- I am chosen by God Almighty and have been adopted into His family forever. (Ephesians 1:3-5)

From the beginning, the Father planned to create a loving family. He has invited us to be part of this family and He longs to enjoy relationship with us. As members of His family, and in order to live victorious Christian lives, it's vital that we know and experience God's immense love for us.

We can have absolute confidence in the truth that, no matter what happens, what we do or fail to do, His passionate, unconditional love for us remains the same. Whether we feel it or not,

His love toward us is utterly unwavering. When a sincere believer stumbles or struggles with sin, God will *never* withhold His love from him or her. He cannot and never will love us less or more than He does right now!

Even our spiritual immaturity does not affect the way God feels towards us. He will love us the same way in heaven—in our perfected resurrection state—as He loves us now. He will never change. He is always 100 percent true to who He is.

For I am the LORD, I do not change; therefore you are not consumed, O sons of Jacob.
Malachi 3:6

Jesus Christ is the same yesterday, today, and forever.
Hebrews 13:8

> "The most remarkable thing has taken place through Christ Jesus. God the Father, Son, and Spirit have opened up the family of God and extended it so that we could come and be a part of it. He did not do this for angels, but only for humans. He does not just love us, but He beckons us to come close to Him, literally to be part of His family forever. The only way that God loves in His family is with all of His heart."
> ~ Mike Bickle

Suggestion: Before completing this study, pray Paul's prayer in Ephesians 3:14-19 for yourself.

> *[14] So when I think of the wisdom of His plan I kneel humbly in awe before the Father of our Lord Jesus, the Messiah, [15] the perfect Father of every father and child in heaven and on the earth. [16] And I pray that He would pour out over you the unlimited riches of His glory and favor until supernatural strength floods your innermost being with his divine might and explosive power.*
>
> *[17] Then, by constantly using your faith, the life of Christ will be released deep inside you, and the resting place of His love will become the very source and root of your life, providing you with a secure foundation that grows and grows.*
>
> *[18-19] Then, as your spiritual strength increases, you will be empowered to discover what every holy one experiences—the great magnitude of the astonishing love of*

Christ in all its dimensions. How deeply intimate and far-reaching is His love!
How enduring and inclusive it is! Endless love beyond measurement, beyond
academic knowledge—this extravagant love pours into you until you are filled to
overflowing with the fullness of God!
Ephesians 3:14-19 (TPT)

⸏

1. How is God's love described in the following Old Testament Scriptures? What do these verses tell you about His love?

Long ago the LORD said to Israel:
   "I have loved you, my people, with an everlasting love.
With unfailing love I have drawn you to myself.
Jeremiah 31:3

Where is another God like you,

who pardons the guilt of the remnant,

overlooking the sins of his special people?

You will not stay angry with your people forever,

because you delight in showing unfailing love.

¹⁹ Once again you will have compassion on us.

You will trample our sins under your feet

and throw them into the depths of the ocean!

Micah 7:18-19

2. From his psalms below, how did King David *feel* about God's love? How do you think experiencing the love of God in these ways affected his actions and his life?

(**Note:** some versions of the Bible translate the word "love" as "loving-kindness" or "mercy.")

But as for me, I will sing about your power.

Each morning I will sing with joy about your unfailing love.

For you have been my refuge,

a place of safety when I am in distress.

¹⁷ O my Strength, to you I sing praises,

for you, O God, are my refuge,

the God who shows me unfailing love.

Psalm 59:16-17

Your unfailing love is better than life itself;
  how I praise you!
Psalm 63:3

He redeems me from death
and crowns me with love and tender mercies.
⁵ *He fills my life with good things.*
My youth is renewed like the eagle's!
⁶ *The LORD gives righteousness*
and justice to all who are treated unfairly
⁷ *He revealed his character to Moses*
and his deeds to the people of Israel.
⁸ *The LORD is compassionate and merciful,*
slow to get angry and filled with unfailing love.
⁹ *He will not constantly accuse us,*
nor remain angry forever.
¹⁰ *He does not punish us for all our sins;*
he does not deal harshly with us, as we deserve.
¹¹ *For his unfailing love toward those who fear him*
is as great as the height of the heavens above the earth.
¹² *He has removed our sins as far from us*
as the east is from the west."

Psalm 103:4-12

❦

"You can give without loving, but you cannot love without giving."
~ Amy Carmichael

3. How does God express His love for us?

For this is how God loved the world: He gave his one and only Son, so that everyone who believes in him will not perish but have eternal life. [17] *God sent his Son into the world not to judge the world, but to save the world through him.*
John 3:16-17

Before the Passover celebration, Jesus knew that his hour had come to leave this world and return to the Father. He had loved his disciples during his ministry on earth, and now he loved them to the very end.
John 13:1

This is real love—not that we loved God, but that he loved us and sent his Son as a sacrifice to take away our sins.
1 John 4:10

4. The night before His crucifixion, what three things did Jesus tell His disciples about His love for them (and for us)?

I have loved you even as the Father has loved me. Remain in my love.
John 15:9

5. What do these verses tell us about our value to God?

6. From John 15:1-8, what do you think it means to "abide" or "remain" in Jesus' love? Practically, how can we do this?

7. What do you think the Holy Spirit's role is in this?

8. What does Jesus' prayer in John 17:22-23 tell us about the Father's love for us?

I have given them the glory you gave me, so they may be one as we are one. [23] I am in them and you are in me. May they experience such perfect unity that the world will know that you sent me and that you love them as much as you love me.
John 17:22-23

9. How can you use these truths in practical ways to combat any lies of the enemy about God's love for you and how He feels towards you, especially when you mess up?

⨕

"God's love for me is perfect because it's based on Him not on me.
So even when I failed He kept loving me." ~ Joyce Meyer, *Beauty for Ashes*

At the last supper, Jesus shares crucial information with His disciples. He knows that within a few short hours He will go to the cross. In John 15:9-11, He tells them about the Father's love, and promises abundant, overflowing joy for those who will abide in His love and obey Him. The deep transforming joy He promises will be more powerful than any fear or temptation the disciples will have to deal with in the devastating events they're about to face.

The same empowering joy Jesus offered His disciples is freely available to us. It is anchored in our revelation of God's love for us and our willingness to abide in that love.

10. What do the following verses say about God's love and our fear?

And as we live in God, our love grows more perfect. So we will not be afraid on the day of judgment, but we can face him with confidence because we live like Jesus here in this world.

[18] Such love has no fear, because perfect love expels all fear. If we are afraid, it is for fear of punishment, and this shows that we have not fully experienced his perfect love.
1 John 4:17-18

11. Are there areas in your life where you deal with fear? In what ways might this be holding you back from becoming all that God wants you to be or from doing all He's called you to do?

Prayer: Ask the Holy Spirit to reveal more of the Father's love for you and show you any areas in your life where insecurity or fear have been or are holding you back from fulfilling God's high calling on your life.

12. From this study so far, what aspects of God's love were especially meaningful to you?

13. In light of this, how can you cooperate with God to become more like Jesus?

Suggestion: When you don't feel loved by God and the devil comes to tell you God doesn't love you because of …, you can answer, "It is written, the Father God loves me in the same way that He loves His Son. Jesus loves me in the same way the Father loves Him. This is the truth! You're a liar, devil, and I refuse to partner with you. I'm standing on the truth of who God says I am and how He sees me!"

> "The sovereign God wants to be loved for Himself and honored for Himself, but that is only part of what He wants. The other part is that He wants us to know that when we have Him we have everything - we have all the rest." ~ A. W. Tozer

B. Chosen by God and Adopted into His Family

"No one can be ordinary when they are in Jesus. It is not allowed!
Heaven comes to us because of our placement in Jesus; not because
of our performance as believers." ~ Graham Cooke

Chosen by God

14. What do the following Old Testament scriptures tell you about God's choice of
    His people Israel?

*The LORD did not set his heart on you and choose you because you were more numerous than
other nations, for you were the smallest of all nations! [8] Rather, it was simply that the LORD
loves you, and he was keeping the oath he had sworn to your ancestors. That is why the LORD
rescued you with such a strong hand from your slavery and from the oppressive hand of
Pharaoh, king of Egypt.*
Deuteronomy 7:7-8

"But you are my witnesses, O Israel!" says the LORD.
   "You are my servant.
You have been chosen to know me, believe in me,
   and understand that I alone am God
There is no other God—
   there never has been, and there never will be."
Isaiah 43:10

15. What can you learn from the following scriptures about when and why God chose these people?

The Prophet Jeremiah

I knew you before I formed you in your mother's womb.
   Before you were born I set you apart
   and appointed you as my prophet to the nations.
Jeremiah 1:5

Jesus' Disciples (and Us)

You didn't choose me. I chose you. I appointed you to go and produce lasting fruit, so that the Father will give you whatever you ask for, using my name.
John 15:16

The Apostle Paul

The Lord said, "Go over to Straight Street, to the house of Judas. When you get there, ask for a man from Tarsus named Saul. He is praying to me right now. *¹² I have shown him a vision of a man named Ananias coming in and laying hands on him so he can see again."*

¹³ "But Lord," exclaimed Ananias, "I've heard many people talk about the terrible things this man has done to the believers in Jerusalem! ¹⁴ And he is authorized by the leading priests to arrest everyone who calls upon your name."

¹⁵ But the Lord said, "Go, for Saul is my chosen instrument to take my message to the Gentiles and to kings, as well as to the people of Israel. ¹⁶ And I will show him how much he must suffer for my name's sake."
Acts 9:11-16

But even before I was born, God chose me and called me by his marvelous grace. Then it pleased him [16] to reveal his Son to me so that I would proclaim the Good News about Jesus to the Gentiles.
Galatians 1:15-16

All of Us

All praise to God, the Father of our Lord Jesus Christ, who has blessed us with every spiritual blessing in the heavenly realms because we are united with Christ. [4] Even before he made the world, God loved us and chose us in Christ to be holy and without fault in his eyes.
Ephesians 1:3-4

16. What do the following verses reveal about your relationship with God now? In light of this, how does He want you to respond?

Since God chose you to be the holy people he loves, you must clothe yourselves with tender-hearted mercy, kindness, humility, gentleness, and patience.
Colossians 3:12

But you are not like that, for you are a chosen people. You are royal priests, a holy nation, God's very own possession. As a result, you can show others the goodness of God, for he called you out of the darkness into his wonderful light.
1 Peter 2:9

Adopted into God's Family

God decided in advance to adopt us into his own family by bringing us to himself through Jesus Christ. This is what he wanted to do, and it gave him great pleasure.
Ephesians 1:5

In order to understand our role as sons (I use this as a generic term, meaning sons or daughters) of Almighty God, it is helpful to see Him as your loving Father. He is the one who chose you to be His child and longs to be known by you as "Abba, ("Papa," "Daddy") Father." Romans 8:15 (Parentheses and words within them have been added.)

Even though God is the almighty, all-powerful creator, He knows and cares deeply about every aspect of your life, loves you passionately and has promised to provide for all your needs. But for better or for worse, the relationship we have or had with our birth father often affects our view of God. So we may need to distinguish between the concept of "father" we learned from our earthly father, and the reality of the true, loving and perfect Father that God is.

❦

The apostle Paul uses the Roman law of adoption to illustrate a Christian's relationship with God. Adoption was not included in the Jewish law and was rarely practiced in Israel, but at that time adoption was quite common in Rome. Lack of a male heir was the main reason for Roman adoptions. Females were almost never adopted and children were seldom adopted. Typically older or adult sons were adopted.

Roman adoptions were taken very seriously. A father had absolute control over his children as long as he lived, no matter how old they were or what positions of influence they'd attained.

A newly adopted son immediately became heir to his father's estate. Upon adoption, he lost all rights to his former natural family and gained all the rights and privileges as a son of his new father. He became a co-heir with any natural born sons in his new family. After his adoption, he was treated as an entirely new person. All debts and obligations related to his family of origin were completely wiped out as if they had never existed.

Paul explains that this is what God has done for us and how He relates to us now as believers in Jesus Christ. Previously we had been members of Adam's family, which included all the effects of sin and guilt. But God adopted us into His family, fully releasing us from all the obligation and debt of sin, which has been fully paid for by Jesus' death on the cross. As adopted children, we now have a new relationship with God that includes all the legal rights of sons. (See Romans 5:12-21.)

> "It was Paul's picture that when a man became a Christian he entered into the very family of God. He did nothing to deserve it; God the great Father in his amazing love and mercy, has taken the lost, helpless, poverty-stricken, debt-laden sinner and adopted him into his own family, so that the debts are cancelled and the glory inherited." ~ William Barclay

17. How does 2 Corinthians 5:17 describe your new status as an adopted son of God?

This means that anyone who belongs to Christ has become a new person. The old life is gone; a new life has begun!

And through the divine authority of His cross, He cancelled out every legal violation we had on our record and the old arrest warrant that stood to indict us. He erased it all—our sins, our stained soul, and our shameful failure to keep His laws—He deleted it all and they cannot be retrieved! Everything we once were in Adam has been placed onto His cross and nailed permanently there as a public display of cancellation!
Colossians 2:14, (TPT)

18. How do you see yourself? Take a few minutes to pause and think about this. What thoughts have you had about yourself today?

19. What or who influenced your answer? Do you tend to define yourself by what you do? Or do you define yourself by what others say or may have said about you or by your successes or failures? Do you tend to see yourself as a sinner or as God's masterpiece?

For we are God's masterpiece. He has created us anew in Christ Jesus, so we can do the good things he planned for us long ago.
Ephesians 2:10

God sees you as His masterpiece! The dictionary defines a masterpiece as, "A work of outstanding artistry, skill or workmanship; an artist or craftsman's finest piece of work." We need to see ourselves as God does; as someone uniquely and skillfully created, precious, beautiful, cherished and unconditionally loved by Him—His favorite.

How do you see yourself? Do you like yourself? We spend a lot of time with ourselves, and it's much more fun to be around those we like and enjoy. How do you relate to yourself? Do you say kind things to yourself?

In today's competitive society, where people are often valued by their achievements and/or appearance, rightly loving ourselves can be challenging. God however looks on the heart (1 Samuel 16:7) and His love isn't based on anything we do or how we look.

Loving ourselves *is* important. We're created to reflect the glory of God, and we are to love others as we love ourselves. So unless we truly love ourselves, not in a selfish, self-indulgent way but in a balanced way, it's impossible to rightly love others.

Because I believe really knowing God's love for me is key, I ask Him daily for more revelation and understanding of His unconditional, extravagant love for me. I know and intellectually believe God loves me, but *feeling* this at a heart level is very different. It affects my spiritual, emotional and physical health. I also ask Him to help me see others with the eyes of His heart.

God not only sees you as His masterpiece, He has also put inside you all the natural talents and spiritual gifts you'll need to accomplish His purpose for you. You are who God says you are. No one, nothing can change that, so don't let the enemy steal your real identity!

Thank you for making me so wonderfully complex!
Your workmanship is marvelous—how well I know it.
Psalm 139:14

"I swell with pride when I can face the whole world and say, 'I belong to Him. The mighty God of this universe is my heavenly Father. I'm His by adoption. I'm a joint-heir with His wonderful Son.' In that moment when you're prone to be depressed, when you find yourself in the spirit of bondage, look up. Just pause and remember to whom you belong." ~ Kathryn Kuhlman

20. What do the following Scriptures tell you about God's Father heart?

Note: This first passage is a picture of God's love for Judah and Jerusalem, but equally depicts His heart for you today.

Never! Can a mother forget her nursing child?
Can she feel no love for the child she has borne?
But even if that were possible,
I would not forget you!
16 See, I have written your name on the palms of my hands.
Always in my mind is a picture of Jerusalem's walls in ruins.
Isaiah 49:15-16

Or if they ask for a fish, do you give them a snake? Of course not! 11 So if you sinful people know how to give good gifts to your children, how much more will your heavenly Father give good gifts to those who ask him.
Matthew 7:10-11

What does the following passage, especially verse 20, tell you about God's Father heart?

To illustrate the point further, Jesus told them this story: "A man had two sons. ¹² The younger son told his father, 'I want my share of your estate now before you die.' So his father agreed to divide his wealth between his sons.

¹³ *"A few days later this younger son packed all his belongings and moved to a distant land, and there he wasted all his money in wild living. ¹⁴ About the time his money ran out, a great famine swept over the land, and he began to starve. ¹⁵ He persuaded a local farmer to hire him, and the man sent him into his fields to feed the pigs. ¹⁶ The young man became so hungry that even the pods he was feeding the pigs looked good to him. But no one gave him anything.*
¹⁷ *"When he finally came to his senses, he said to himself, 'At home even the hired servants have food enough to spare, and here I am dying of hunger! ¹⁸ I will go home to my father and say, "Father, I have sinned against both heaven and you, ¹⁹ and I am no longer worthy of being called your son. Please take me on as a hired servant."'*

²⁰ *"So he returned home to his father. And while he was still a long way off, his father saw him coming. Filled with love and compassion, he ran to his son, embraced him, and kissed him.*
²¹ *His son said to him, 'Father, I have sinned against both heaven and you, and I am no longer worthy of being called your son.'*

²² *"But his father said to the servants, 'Quick! Bring the finest robe in the house and put it on him. Get a ring for his finger and sandals for his feet. ²³ And kill the calf we have been fattening. We must celebrate with a feast, ²⁴ for this son of mine was dead and has now returned to life. He was lost, but now he is found.' So the party began."*
Luke 15:11-24

21. Reflect on what you just wrote. What feelings are you experiencing?

22. What aspects of God as your Father do you find easiest to accept? Most difficult? Why?

23. What is most meaningful to you about being chosen by God and/or adopted into His family?

24. In light of this, ask the Holy Spirit if there are any changes He would like you to make in your life. Write them below.

"He remembers our frame and knows that we are dust. He may sometimes chasten us, it is true, but even this He does with a smile, the proud, tender smile of a Father who is bursting with pleasure over an imperfect but promising son who is coming every day to look more and more like the One whose child he is." ~ A.W. Tozer

You have seen how you are loved, chosen and adopted into God's royal family. In Study Three you'll learn how to effectively use the truth of God's Word to triumph over debilitating lies and truly reign in life!

"You were placed here to train for eternity." ~ J.C. Ryle

Prayer Requests and Notes

_____

_____

_____

_____

_____

_____

_____

_____

_____

_____

_____

_____

_____

_____

_____

_____

_____

_____

_____

_____

Study Three
Reigning in Life

A. Reigning in Life Every Day

He … raised us up with Him, and seated us with Him in the heavenly places in Christ Jesus, [7] so that in the ages to come He might show the surpassing riches of His grace in kindness toward us in Christ Jesus.
Ephesians 2:6–7 (NASB)

"This is remarkable. Paul is emphasizing this point that we will sit on thrones, and we will rule with Him. In verse six he explains that Jesus made us to sit together in heavenly places." ~ Mike Bickle

Declarations:

- I am a royal daughter/son of the Lord God Almighty. (John 1:12)

- Jesus Christ invites me to reign with Him forever! (Revelation 3:21)

- In Christ I am more than a conqueror. (Romans 8:37)

God has granted us the amazing privilege of not only being part of His family, we are His royal sons and daughters, which in itself is astounding. More than that, He tells us that He also longs for us to be close to Him forever; actually reigning with Him for all eternity.

... and from Jesus Christ. He is the faithful witness to these things, the first to rise from the dead, and the ruler of all the kings of the world.

All glory to him who loves us and has freed us from our sins by shedding his blood for us. He has made us a Kingdom of priests for God his Father. All glory and power to him forever and ever! Amen.
~ Revelation 1:5-6

To him who overcomes I will grant to sit with Me on My throne, as I also overcame and sat down with My Father on His throne.
~ Revelation 3:21 (NKJV)

1. Prayerfully read and think about the above scriptures. What has God promised regarding your status in the ages to come? How do you feel about this? How might knowing this affect the way you look at life now and how you live each day?

2. From Ephesians 2:6-7, what do you think it means to be seated with Christ now in the heavenly realms? How might believing this cause you to change the way you think or act today? What will this reveal about God in the coming age (verse 7)?

3. How does Daniel 7:27 describe the future role of God's people?

Then the sovereignty, power, and greatness of all the kingdoms under heaven will be given to the holy people of the Most High. His kingdom will last forever, and all rulers will serve and obey him.

Training a Princess

Queen Elizabeth II became heir apparent to the throne when she was ten years old. She was in the direct line of succession after her father. As a child, Elizabeth was groomed and trained for her royal role. She was educated by tutors at home with her younger sister. She also received tuition from her father, as well as sessions with the Vice-Provost of Eton (Eton College is an elite boys' boarding school near Windsor in England) and she was instructed in religion by the Archbishop of Canterbury.

In her role as Princess Elizabeth, she also learned French from a number of French and Belgian governesses. She has used this skill as Queen when speaking to ambassadors and heads of state from French-speaking countries, and when visiting French-speaking provinces in Canada. Elizabeth was carefully and thoroughly trained. She studied hard for her royal role as queen. How much more should we, as sons and daughters of the King, invest time and energy to learn to walk fully in our royal calling?

4. Think about and picture how your life would be different if you had been raised in a palace as a prince or princess being groomed to be king or queen.
    In what ways would you see yourself differently than you do now?
    In order to be a successful king, what new thoughts and/or beliefs would you need to adopt?

5. In light of your answers above, ask the Holy Spirit to show you any beliefs, mindsets and/or behaviors He would like you to change in order to more fully walk out your royal calling. Write these below.

"Kingdom life, eternal life, flows directly from knowing God personally. Our relationship with God is the key to 'reigning in life,' because it is in coming to know Him that we come to know who we are, what our purpose in life is, and how to walk it out. As we align our thinking and behavior with who He is, the supernatural life of His kingdom begins to flow through our lives, enabling us to do what we could not otherwise do."

~ Kris Vallotton, *Basic Training for the Supernatural Ways of Royalty*

We have dual citizenship. We are first of all citizens of heaven even now and we are also citizens of wherever we live on earth. We represent heaven here on earth.

6. In the following verses, what hope does Paul give his readers regarding their future? In what ways might this promise be an encouragement to you today? What might it mean in practical terms to live as a citizen of heaven on earth?

But we are citizens of heaven, where the Lord Jesus Christ lives. And we are eagerly waiting for him to return as our Savior. [21] He will take our weak mortal bodies and change them into glorious bodies like his own, using the same power with which he will bring everything under his control.
Philippians 3:20-21

7. What can you learn from the following scriptures about who you are in Christ and what He has done for you?

But to all who believed him and accepted him, he gave the right to become children of God.
John 1:12

This means that anyone who belongs to Christ has become a new person. The old life is gone; a new life has begun!
2 Corinthians 5:17

So now you Gentiles are no longer strangers and foreigners. You are citizens along with all of God's holy people. You are members of God's family.
Ephesians 2:19

For he has rescued us from the kingdom of darkness and transferred us into the Kingdom of his dear Son, [14] who purchased our freedom and forgave our sins.
Colossians 1:13-14

"Sonship is a thing which all the infirmities of our flesh, and all the sins into which we are hurried by temptation, can never violate or weaken." ~ Charles H. Spurgeon

B. Truth Triumphs Over Lies

Even though we're royal sons and daughters of the King, we are engaged in an on-going battle. This battle is fought primarily in our minds, which is where the enemy usually attacks us. He is determined to try and keep us from being effective for God and His Kingdom. His primary weapon is deception. However, we have God's powerful truth—His Word—that breaks the power of lies.

Some years ago I experienced the truth of this. I´d become ill and was crippled. Because of this, I'd lost most everything I owned: my home, my business, and my freedom. I was dependent on others to help me. I was in a lot of pain and I didn´t know what would become of me or what I was going to do next. It was scary.

Because of the pain, I couldn´t sleep more than a couple of hours at a time. Not being able to sleep night after night is no fun. The devil would mess with my mind during those long, sleepless nights. I became too exhausted and weak to fight back. I knew God cared, but I wasn't sure what to do.

I felt I had to do something or go crazy. I knew that God´s Word, the Bible, was the key. Even Jesus when confronted by the devil responded, "It is written…" So, in order to keep my sanity, I chose and recorded some verses of scripture. Then, instead of tossing and turning and worrying during those seemingly endless hours in the night, just waiting for morning, I could listen to God´s promises.

Among others, I chose Scriptures and promises about who I am in Christ. For example, "I am a child of God" (John 1:12); "I'm blessed in the heavenly realms with every spiritual blessing"

(Ephesians 1:3); "I'm adopted as God's child" (Ephesians 1:5); and more. I created, recorded and listened for hours to a long, long list of these promises.

I learned in a very practical way how the power of God's truth really does overcome the lies of the enemy.

The devil doesn't want us to receive God's love or know and walk in who He has created and destined us to be. He uses deception to his advantage whenever he can. His lies can create a filter that distorts our understanding of who God is, preventing us from experiencing His love and believing who we really are in Him.

> "The major strategy of Satan is to distort the character of God and the truth of who we are. He can't change God and he can't do anything to change our identity and position in Christ. If, however, he can get us to believe a lie, we will live as though our identity in Christ isn't true." ~ Neil T. Anderson

Note: The devil's deceptive thoughts or lies typically come in the first person singular in a way that we think they're our own thoughts.

8. As He addresses the religious leaders who were vehemently opposed to Him, how does Jesus describe the devil in John 8:44?

For you are the children of your father the devil, and you love to do the evil things he does. He was a murderer from the beginning. He has always hated the truth, because there is no truth in him. When he lies, it is consistent with his character; for he is a liar and the father of lies.

DISCOVER THE ROYAL YOU!

9. What can you learn from Revelation 12:9 and 1 John 5:19 about the devil and his effect on the world?

This great dragon—the ancient serpent called the devil, or Satan, the one deceiving the whole world—was thrown down to the earth with all his angels.
Revelation 12:9

We know that we are children of God and that the world around us is under the control of the evil one.
1 John 5:19

10. In Matthew 4:1-11, how did Jesus respond to the lies of the devil? What can you learn from this that will help you when he tempts you to believe lies?

11. How do the following scriptures describe your position in this battle? What promises do they give that you can claim?

What shall we say about such wonderful things as these? If God is for us, who can ever be against us? ³² Since he did not spare even his own Son but gave him up for us all, won't he also give us everything else? ³³ Who dares accuse us whom God has chosen for his own? No one—for God himself has given us right standing with himself. ³⁴ Who then will condemn us? No one— for Christ Jesus died for us and was raised to life for us, and he is sitting in the place of honor at God's right hand, pleading for us.

³⁵ Can anything ever separate us from Christ's love? Does it mean he no longer loves us if we have trouble or calamity, or are persecuted, or hungry, or destitute, or in danger, or threatened with death? ³⁶ (As the Scriptures say, "For your sake we are killed every day; we are being slaughtered like sheep.") ³⁷ No, despite all these things, overwhelming victory is ours through Christ, who loved us.
Romans 8:31-37

But you belong to God, my dear children. You have already won a victory over those people, because the Spirit who lives in you is greater than the spirit who lives in the world.
1 John 4:4

We know that God's children do not make a practice of sinning, for God's Son holds them securely, and the evil one cannot touch them.
1 John 5:18

12. What does 1 Peter 5:8-9 warn about the enemy? What should your response to him be?

⁸Stay alert! Watch out for your great enemy, the devil. He prowls around like a roaring lion, looking for someone to devour. ⁹ Stand firm against him, and be strong in your faith. Remember that your family of believers all over the world is going through the same kind of suffering you are.
1 Peter 5:8-9

Note: The devil is *not* a lion, he simply prowls around like one. We do have a victorious Lion (Revelation 5:5).

DISCOVER THE ROYAL YOU!

Three Simple Steps to Overcome Lies

Step 1 – Expose the lie. Acknowledge it, bring it out into the light of day and name it for what it is.

Step 2 – Renounce the lie. A definition of renounce: "Give up by formal declaration, disown, reject as having no authority." For example, after exposing a lie you've believed, you might say something like, "I'm aware that … is simply not true. I refuse to believe or entertain that thought anymore and I renounce it as a lie."

Step 3 – Replace the lie. Find a truth from God's Word which states the opposite of the lie you believed and affirm your faith in this truth.

Three Common Lies and Truths that Triumph Over Them

- Fear and anxiety
- Failure to believe God really loves you
- Forgiveness isn't important

• **Fear and anxiety** – A definition of fear: "A distressing emotion aroused by impending danger, evil, pain, etc., whether the threat is real or imagined."

Satan frequently uses fear to take people's attention away from God, stopping them from fulfilling their destiny and from enjoying life.

Anything you fear more than God is an idol. You've made it more powerful than Him!

"Worry is meditating on the lies of the devil."

13. In Philippians 4:6-7, what does Paul tell his readers to do when they become anxious and fearful?

Don't worry about anything; instead, pray about everything. Tell God what you need, and thank him for all he has done. ⁷ *Then you will experience God's peace, which exceeds anything we can understand. His peace will guard your hearts and minds as you live in Christ Jesus.*

14. Knowing that in a few short hours His disciples will be tempted to extreme fear and confusion, what does Jesus tell them in John 14:27 and 16:33? How could you apply these truths in your life when you're tempted to fear?

I am leaving you with a gift—peace of mind and heart. And the peace I give is a gift the world cannot give. So don't be troubled or afraid.
John 14:27

I have told you all this so that you may have peace in me. Here on earth you will have many trials and sorrows. But take heart, because I have overcome the world.
John 16:33

"To win the war against fear, we must know the true God as He is revealed in the Bible. He works to give us lasting peace. He receives joy, not from condemning us but in rescuing us from the devil. Yes, the Lord will bring conviction to our hearts concerning sin, but it is so He can deliver us from sin's power and consequences. In its place, the Lord works to establish healing, forgiveness and peace." ~ Francis Frangipane

- **Failure to believe God really loves you** – Even though we've read and believed that God loves us, when we make a foolish mistake, we can be tempted to believe the lie that, "God can't possibly have the same heart of love towards me now after what I've done." We may even bargain with Him and somehow try to make up for what we did, promising never to do it again.

15. What do John 10:28-29, Romans 8:1-2 and 38-39 say about how God feels about you?

I give them eternal life, and they will never perish. No one can snatch them away from me, [29] for my Father has given them to me, and he is more powerful than anyone else. No one can snatch them from the Father's hand.
John 10:28-29

So now there is no condemnation for those who belong to Christ Jesus. And because you belong to him, the power of the life-giving Spirit has freed you from the power of sin that leads to death.
Romans 8:1-2

And I am convinced that nothing can ever separate us from God's love. Neither death nor life, neither angels nor demons, neither our fears for today nor our worries about tomorrow—not even the powers of hell can separate us from God's love. [39] No power in the sky above or in the earth below—indeed, nothing in all creation will ever be able to separate us from the love of God that is revealed in Christ Jesus our Lord.
Romans 8:38-39

16. Take some time to meditate on Romans 6:4-7. Ask the Holy Spirit to show you new dimensions of this familiar truth and ways you can experience His power.

For we died and were buried with Christ by baptism. And just as Christ was raised from the dead by the glorious power of the Father, now we also may live new lives.

⁵ Since we have been united with him in his death, we will also be raised to life as he was. ⁶ We know that our old sinful selves were crucified with Christ so that sin might lose its power in our lives. We are no longer slaves to sin. ⁷ For when we died with Christ we were set free from the power of sin.
Romans 6:4-7

- **Forgiveness isn't important** – A favorite deception of the devil is to bring to mind unkind things people have said or done to us. Then, instead of forgiving those who wronged or hurt us, he tempts us to review and mull over these instances in our minds.

It's easy to dismiss forgiveness as unimportant, but Satan knows that if we fail to forgive, it will block our relationship with God. Unforgiveness can also result in bitterness and resentment, which in turn can even cause physical illness.

Forgive anyone you need to forgive, including yourself. You may even need to forgive God if you are angry with Him for some reason—maybe because your life just isn't the way you think it should be. You might need to forgive a company or store that may have cheated you, an organization, a church or a bank, etc.

Truly forgiving others and ourselves helps to break any agreement with a lie.

"After helping thousands find their freedom in Christ, I can testify that unforgiveness is the major reason people remain in bondage to the past."

~ Neil T. Anderson

17.   Ask God to bring to mind anyone you need to forgive and forgive them now. This isn't always a onetime event. When the enemy brings it up again, determine to quickly forgive them again and again, if necessary.

In Luke 6:27-28, how does Jesus tell you to respond to those who hurt you?

But to you who are willing to listen, I say, love your enemies! Do good to those who hate you. [28] *Bless those who curse you. Pray for those who hurt you.*

"Forgiveness is an act of the will, and the will can function regardless of the temperature of the heart." ~ Corrie Ten Boom

18. This battle with the enemy is fought mainly in your mind and you choose what you think about. In view of this, how can you practically apply Paul's challenge to his readers in Philippians 4:8-9?

And now, dear brothers and sisters, one final thing. Fix your thoughts on what is true, and honorable, and right, and pure, and lovely, and admirable. Think about things that are excellent and worthy of praise. ⁹ Keep putting into practice all you learned and received from me— everything you heard from me and saw me doing. Then the God of peace will be with you.

19. What does the Apostle John say about sin and forgiveness in 1 John 1:8-10 and 2:1-2?

If we claim we have no sin, we are only fooling ourselves and not living in the truth. ⁹ But if we confess our sins to him, he is faithful and just to forgive us our sins and to cleanse us from all wickedness. ¹⁰ If we claim we have not sinned, we are calling God a liar and showing that his word has no place in our hearts.
1 John 1:8-10

My dear children, I am writing this to you so that you will not sin. But if anyone does sin, we have an advocate who pleads our case before the Father. He is Jesus Christ, the one who is truly righteous. ² He himself is the sacrifice that atones for our sins—and not only our sins but the sins of all the world.
1 John 2:1-2

20. Ask the Holy Spirit to show you any lies you are currently believing in any area of your life. Write down each lie and think about how believing the lie has affected your emotions and actions.

Ask the Holy Spirit to show you what truth(s) will conquer each of these lies, and write them down.

Lie

For example:
I feel like a failure, I'm discouraged
and I don't want to try again.

Truth

– *God sees me as more than a conqueror*
Romans 8:37. I can do this in Christ's
strength – Philippians 4:13

_____ – _____

_____ – _____

_____ – _____

_____ – _____

_____ – _____

_____ – _____

_____ – _____

We are to keep our focus and attention on the Lord Jesus Christ and not on the enemy, but scripture cautions us not to be ignorant of his schemes. As a lover of God, as His royal son or daughter, you have a high calling on your life. My prayer is that you will fully live out your royal calling in Christ without any unnecessary distractions or compromises. For that reason, I've devoted much of this Bible study and the next one to exposing some of the devil's strategies in order to help you avoid them and to become and do all that God has destined and called you to be and do.

This resurrection life you received from God is not a timid, grave-tending life. It's adventurously expectant, greeting God with a childlike "What's next, Papa?" God's Spirit touches our spirits and confirms who we really are. We know who he is, and we know who we are: Father and children. And we know we are going to get what's coming to us—an unbelievable inheritance! We go through exactly what Christ goes through. If we go through the hard times with him, then we're certainly going to go through the good times with him!
Romans 8:15-17 (MSG)

As His royal son or daughter, God has given you authority. In the next study, you'll learn about spiritual warfare, faith, and how to appropriately exercise your God-given authority.

"Only those who are spiritual perceive the reality of the spiritual foe and hence engage in battle. Such warfare is not fought with arms of the flesh. Because the conflict is spiritual so must be the weapons." ~ Watchman Nee

Prayer Requests and Notes

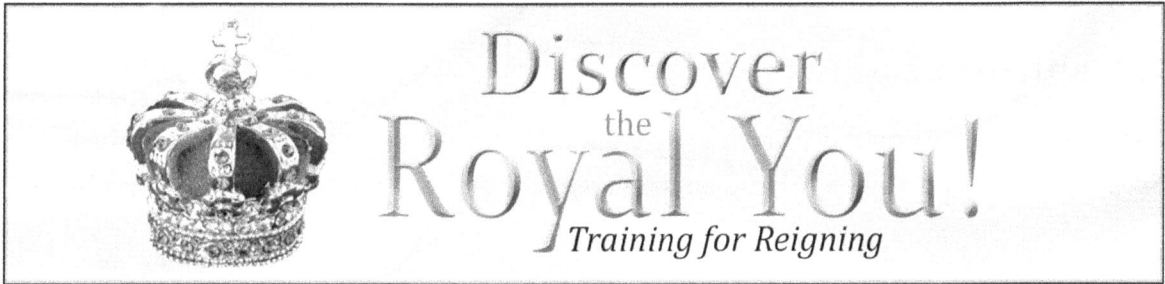
Discover the Royal You!
Training for Reigning

Study Four
The Royal Scepter – Your Authority in Christ

A. Authority Stolen

"To some, the image of a pale body glimmering on a dark night whispers of defeat. What good is a God who does not control his Son's suffering? But another sound can be heard: the shout of a God crying out to human beings, 'I LOVE YOU.' Love was compressed for all history in that lonely figure on the cross, who said that he could call down angels at any moment on a rescue mission, but chose not to – because of us. At Calvary, God accepted his own unbreakable terms of justice." ~ Philip Yancey

Declarations:

- God's measureless resurrection power is available to me by faith! (Ephesians 1:19-20)

- God completely erased all record of my sins on the cross. They're deleted and cannot be retrieved! (Colossians 2:14)

- I've been given power in Jesus' name over all demons and to heal all diseases. (Luke 9:1)

Definitions:

Authority: power or right delegated or given. Its value depends on the force behind the user.
Scepter: a rod or staff given to a monarch as a symbol of the authority invested in him or her.

Suggestion: before completing this study, take a few minutes to read through and pray Paul's prayer in Ephesians 1:17-23 for yourself.

And I pray continually that the Father of Glory, the God of our Lord Jesus Christ, would unveil in you the riches of the spirit of wisdom and the spirit of revelation through the fullness of being one with Christ.

[18] I pray that the light of God will brighten the eyes of your innermost being, flooding you with light, until you experience the full revelation of our great hope of glory. We know that is the reason He called you to Himself. And I pray that you will truly experience all the riches of this wealth that has been freely given to all His holy ones, for you are His true inheritance!

[19] Yes, my prayer for you is that every moment you will experience the measureless power of God made available to you through faith. Then your lives will be an advertisement of this immense power as it works through you!

[20] This is the resurrection power that was released through Christ when God raised Him from the dead. This resurrection power raised us up and seated us with Him at His place of supreme authority in the heavenly realm!

[21] And now He is exalted higher than all the thrones and principalities, above every ruler and authority, and above every realm of power there is! He is gloriously enthroned over every name that is ever praised, not only in this age, but in the age that is coming!

[22] And everything now finds its essence in Him, and He alone is the Leader and Source of everything needed in the church. God has put everything beneath the authority of Jesus Christ and has given Him the highest rank above all others! [23] And now we, His church, are His body on the earth and the completion of Him that fills all things with His presence flowing through us!
Ephesians 1:17-23 (TPT)

1. In verses 19 and 20, what does Paul pray for these believers? What does this passage say about your position in Christ? What kind of power has God made available to you? How can you make use of this power now?

2. In what area of your life do you need to experience this power today? Are you facing a seemingly insurmountable challenge? Do you find yourself in a situation for which you feel inadequate? If so, describe it below.

3. Considering the measureless power of God made available to you through faith, how are you asking God to work in the situation(s) in your life you just wrote about? What do you need that could bring a solution?

4. Write in your own words what verses 20-23 say about Jesus.

༄

In Genesis 1:26-28 we read that God created man in His own image and gave him authority; principal leadership over the earth. However, when man sinned by believing Satan's lie and following him instead of obeying God, he transferred the authority God had given him to Satan. (See Genesis 2:15-17 and 3:1-7.)

5.   What do Psalm 8:4-6 and Psalm 115:16 reveal about God's intended role for people?

⁴ What are mere mortals that you should think about them,
    human beings that you should care for them?
⁵ Yet you made them only a little lower than God
    and crowned them with glory and honor.
⁶ You gave them charge of everything you made,
    putting all things under their authority
Psalm 8:4-6

The heavens belong to our God, they are His alone,
    But He has given us the earth and put us in charge!
Psalm 115:16 (TPT)

6. When tempting Jesus (before the cross), what did the devil say in this passage about his authority on the earth?

Then the devil took him up and revealed to him all the kingdoms of the world in a moment of time. [6] *"I will give you the glory of these kingdoms and authority over them," the devil said, "because they are mine to give to anyone I please. I will give it all to you if you will worship me."*
Luke 4:5-6

B. Authority Restored

God is a perfectly just, judicial God. A man had given away his authority to rule over the earth, and only a man—a perfect, sinless man—could legally purchase it back. Jesus did this on the cross, taking back authority over the earth.

Jesus came up and said to them, "All authority (all power of absolute rule) in heaven and on earth has been given to Me."
Matthew 28:18 (AMP)

"Life is wasted if we do not grasp the glory of the cross, cherish it for the treasure that it is, and cleave to it as the highest price of every pleasure and the deepest comfort in every pain. What was once foolishness to us— a crucified God—must become our wisdom and our power and our only boast in this world." ~ John Piper

7. Prayerfully read Colossians 2:11-15. What does this tell you about your standing with God in both the past and the present? What has He done for you (verse 14)? How does verse 15 describe what happened to Satan's domain?

When you came to Christ, you were "circumcised," but not by a physical procedure. Christ performed a spiritual circumcision—the cutting away of your sinful nature. [12] For you were buried with Christ when you were baptized. And with him you were raised to new life because you trusted the mighty power of God, who raised Christ from the dead.

[13] You were dead because of your sins and because your sinful nature was not yet cut away. Then God made you alive with Christ, for he forgave all our sins. [14] He canceled the record of the charges against us and took it away by nailing it to the cross. [15] In this way, he disarmed the spiritual rulers and authorities. He shamed them publicly by his victory over them on the cross.

All authority belongs to God. Jesus isn't here in flesh as a person now, but He has delegated His authority on earth to us, His body, the Church. He has commissioned us to be His representatives and to enforce His authority on earth. He exercises His authority through us.

However in order to exercise the authority He has given us, He requires that we are rightly submitted to and honor authority ourselves in families (Matthew 19:19, Colossians 3:18-22); our places of employment (Ephesians 6:5-8); the civil government (Romans 13:1-7); and in the church (1 Timothy 5:17).

✍

"His authority on earth allows us to dare to go to all the nations. His authority in heaven gives us our only hope of success. And His presence with us leaves us no other choice." ~ John Stott

8. In Matthew 28:18-20, what does Jesus tell His disciples about His authority? On the basis of this, what three things are they to do? What do you think it means to "make disciples"? How does what He told the disciples apply to you today? What does He promise His disciples (and you)?

Jesus came and told his disciples, "I have been given all authority in heaven and on earth. [19] Therefore, go and make disciples of all the nations, baptizing them in the name of the Father and the Son and the Holy Spirit. [20] Teach these new disciples to obey all the commands I have given you. And be sure of this: I am with you always, even to the end of the age."

9. According to 2 Corinthians 5:18-19 and Ephesians 6:18, what else are we commissioned
    to do?

*And all of this is a gift from God, who brought us back to himself through Christ. And God has
given us this task of reconciling people to him. ¹⁹ For God was in Christ, reconciling the world to
himself, no longer counting people's sins against them. And he gave us this wonderful message of
reconciliation.*
2 Corinthians 5:18-19

*Pray in the Spirit at all times and on every occasion. Stay alert and be persistent in your prayers
for all believers everywhere.*
Ephesians 6:18

C. Exercise Your Authority

Over What Are We Given Authority?

It's important that we remain aware of who we are in Christ and the authority He has delegated to us; also that this authority comes from Christ's resurrection and exaltation. It is based solely on what He has accomplished and does not depend on anything we have achieved, our mood or on how we may feel. Yet it's impossible to fully comprehend this authority with our intellect alone, we need spiritual revelation to really understand it.

Suggestion: Ask the Holy Spirit to give you a greater revelation of your authority in Christ.

10. From the following scriptures, over what did Jesus give the disciples (and us) authority in Luke 9:1 and 10:19? In what circumstances and how are you to use this power?

One day Jesus called together his twelve disciples and gave them power and authority to cast out all demons and to heal all diseases.
Luke 9:1

Look, I have given you authority over all the power of the enemy, and you can walk among snakes and scorpions and crush them. Nothing will injure you.
Luke 10:19

Note: 'Serpents and scorpions' refer to the power of unclean, demonic spirits. (Psalm 91:13) Demons have to obey the authority of Jesus through us. We shouldn't fear them and they're certainly not afraid of us, but they do fear and must obey Jesus Christ whom we represent.

⸙

Our Faith and Authority

11. In Mark 4:35-40, over what did Jesus demonstrate His authority? Why do you think He reprimanded the disciples for their lack of faith?

35 As evening came, Jesus said to his disciples, "Let's cross to the other side of the lake." 36 So they took Jesus in the boat and started out, leaving the crowds behind (although other boats followed). 37 But soon a fierce storm came up. High waves were breaking into the boat, and it began to fill with water.

38 Jesus was sleeping at the back of the boat with his head on a cushion. The disciples woke him up, shouting, "Teacher, don't you care that we're going to drown?"

39 When Jesus woke up, he rebuked the wind and said to the waves, "Silence! Be still!" Suddenly the wind stopped, and there was a great calm. 40 Then he asked them, "Why are you afraid? Do you still have no faith?"

Mark 4:35-40

12. What can you learn about Jesus' authority, your authority and faith from Matthew 21:18-22?

In the morning, as Jesus was returning to Jerusalem, he was hungry, ¹⁹ and he noticed a fig tree beside the road. He went over to see if there were any figs, but there were only leaves. Then he said to it, "May you never bear fruit again!" And immediately the fig tree withered up.

²⁰ The disciples were amazed when they saw this and asked, "How did the fig tree wither so quickly?"

²¹ Then Jesus told them, "I tell you the truth, if you have faith and don't doubt, you can do things like this and much more. You can even say to this mountain, 'May you be lifted up and thrown into the sea,' and it will happen. ²² You can pray for anything, and if you have faith, you will receive it."
Matthew 21:18-22

13. What might prevent you from appropriately using your authority?

14. How do Acts 10:38 and 1 John 3:8 describe what Jesus did on earth?

And you know that God anointed Jesus of Nazareth with the Holy Spirit and with power. Then Jesus went around doing good and healing all who were oppressed by the devil, for God was with him.
Acts 10:38

But when people keep on sinning, it shows that they belong to the devil, who has been sinning since the beginning. But the Son of God came to destroy the works of the devil.
1 John 3:8

⚮

Authority and Spiritual Warfare

Whether we like it or not, or choose to acknowledge it or not—if we have trusted Christ as our Savior and Lord, we're in a war. This is a spiritual battle that can only be won using spiritual weapons. There is no 'cease fire' in this conflict!

> "As Christians, we wage most of our 'warfare' by doing things that don't look like fighting. We prophesy blessing and destiny over people and cities. We love people sacrificially and bless them when they curse us. We pray for Heaven to come to earth." ~ Kris Vallotton

15. According to Ephesians 6:12 who are we fighting against?

For we are not fighting against flesh-and-blood enemies, but against evil rulers and authorities of the unseen world, against mighty powers in this dark world, and against evil spirits in the heavenly places.

16. What do Jesus' words in John 10:10 tell you about His and the devil's objectives in this battle?

The thief's purpose is to steal and kill and destroy. My purpose is to give them a rich and satisfying life.

As His royal sons and daughters, God has called us to enforce Jesus' authority on the earth. Satan's attacks will continue if we do nothing to stop them. We must use our authority against him. God won't do this for us.

17. In the following scriptures, what are you asked to do? What do you think it means in practical terms to follow these instructions?

So humble yourselves before God. Resist the devil, and he will flee from you.
James 4:7

Stay alert! Watch out for your great enemy, the devil. He prowls around like a roaring lion, looking for someone to devour. ⁹ Stand firm against him, and be strong in your faith. Remember that your family of believers all over the world is going through the same kind of suffering you are.
1 Peter 5:8-9

Therefore, put on every piece of God's armor so you will be able to resist the enemy in the time of evil. Then after the battle you will still be standing firm. [14] Stand your ground, putting on the belt of truth and the body armor of God's righteousness. [15] For shoes, put on the peace that comes from the Good News so that you will be fully prepared. [16] In addition to all of these, hold up the shield of faith to stop the fiery arrows of the devil. [17] Put on salvation as your helmet, and take the sword of the Spirit, which is the word of God.

[18] *Pray in the Spirit at all times and on every occasion. Stay alert and be persistent in your prayers for all believers everywhere.*
Ephesians 6:13-18

18. What does 2 Corinthians 10:3-5 tell you about this battle? Where and how is the battle primarily fought?

We are human, but we don't wage war as humans do. ⁴ We use God's mighty weapons, not worldly weapons, to knock down the strongholds of human reasoning and to destroy false arguments. ⁵ We destroy every proud obstacle that keeps people from knowing God. We capture their rebellious thoughts and teach them to obey Christ.

"Any battle for victory, power, and deliverance - from ourselves and from sin - which is not based constantly upon the gazing and the beholding of the Lord Jesus, with the heart and life lifted up to Him, is doomed to failure."
~ Alan Redpath

DISCOVER THE ROYAL YOU!

19. One of the devil's main strategies in this conflict is to distract us and divert our focus away from God, from loving and obeying Him. How have you seen the devil do this in your life? What are some ways you've been alerted to recognize this and overcome it?

✑

We Wage War with Words

Words carry power. In Genesis 1 we read that God spoke the world into existence. The words we speak affect us and those who hear them. Our words can increase faith or fear! They can bless or curse!

When our spirit and our words agree with God's Word, they will release His power. But if we speak in agreement with Satan's accusations, we release his power in our lives.

Our words affect what happens in the spirit realm. Matthew 16:19 states that we have been given the keys of authority in Jesus' name to stop (bind) demonic activity and to release (loose) God's power—to bring heaven to earth.

20. What does Proverbs 18:21 say about spoken words? In what ways do you think your words could harm or bless?

Words kill, words give life;
* they're either poison or fruit—you choose.*
Proverbs 18:21 (MSG)

21. In John 6:63, what did Jesus say about His own words?

The Spirit alone gives eternal life. Human effort accomplishes nothing. And the very words I have spoken to you are spirit and life.

Note: We may not always see immediate victory; we need to exercise both faith and patience. (See Hebrews 6:12.)

> "There is no neutral ground in the universe; every square inch, every split second, is claimed by God and counter-claimed by Satan." ~ C.S. Lewis

Be Ready to Use Your Authority!

Two of the enemy's most effective tools against us are fear and unworthiness. Both come as thoughts that divert our attention away from God and His purposes. Both are debilitating and make us feel miserable.

When we're fearful and/or anxious, the enemy will often use "what if…" thoughts that send us imagining all kinds of disastrous possibilities. We must learn to quickly recognize these thoughts and refuse to entertain and partner with them. God doesn't want us to live in torment; His plan for us is to live in peace.

When starting something new, or speaking in front of a group of people, I almost always deal with fear. I don't like it, but I decided long ago never to let it to stop me from doing what I believe God wants me to do. It's often scary, but I choose to turn my focus onto Him and who He is. I ask for a greater revelation of how totally good He is and how very much He loves me. This gives me the courage to go on, even in the face of fear.

Fear begins with a thought, which usually stirs up stressful emotions. We have a choice: we can let these thoughts roll around in our mind, or we can use our authority in Jesus' name to rebuke the enemy—tell him to leave. Then we must turn our thoughts to focus on God's promises. For instance Philippians 4:6-7 instructs, *Don't worry about anything; instead, pray about everything; tell God your needs, and don't forget to thank him for his answers. If you do this, you will experience God's peace, which is far more wonderful than the human mind can understand. His peace will keep your thoughts and your hearts quiet and at rest as you trust in Christ Jesus.* (TLB)

Unworthiness is another of the enemy's favorite weapons against us. As with fear, he works in our minds, planting thoughts of condemnation and shame. Without Jesus' blood, none of us can stand before a holy God. We all have a long list of sins of which we're very aware. The devil delights in reminding us of these and of how pitiful and undeserving we are. He knows that if he can get us focused on our faults and failures, we won't be a problem to him. However scripture tells us that when we've confessed out sin God doesn't remember it. He has wiped our slate clean.

For in the Son all our sins are cancelled and we have the release of redemption through the ransom price He paid—His very blood.
Colossians 1:14 (TPT)

When the devil comes with any of these thoughts, we need to quickly recognize what is going on, use our authority to rebuke the enemy, and remind ourselves of who we are in Christ—God's royal child—His favorite!

⌘

22. In light of what you've learned about your authority in Christ, what areas of your life do you feel God is asking you to grow in this authority? How will you do that?

"Jesus defeated satan in Gethsemane on the cross, not by directly confronting the devil, but by fulfilling the destiny to which He had been called. The greatest battle that was ever won was accomplished by the apparent death of the victor, without even a word of rebuke to His adversary!" ~ Francis Frangipane

God invites you to enjoy rewarding, authentic friendships with Himself and with others, but this doesn't happen without your conscious involvement. The next study deals with some practical ways to develop and deepen fulfilling relationships with God and with those around you.

"Friendship is the source of the greatest pleasures, and without friends even the most agreeable pursuits become tedious. There is nothing on this earth more to be prized than true friendship." ~ Thomas Aquinas

Prayer Requests and Notes

_____

_____

_____

_____

_____

_____

_____

_____

_____

_____

_____

_____

_____

_____

_____

_____

_____

_____

_____

Study Five
Royal Relationships

A. Relating to the Godhead – Father, Son and Holy Spirit

"Four of the Ten Commandments deal with our relationship to God while the other six deal with our relationships with people. But all ten are about relationships."
~ Rick Warren

Declarations:

- God loves me passionately and I love Him in return. (1 John 4:19)

- I obey God and enjoy living in His love for me. (John 15:10)

- I consistently recognize the glory in others and honor them. (Romans 12:10)

Intimacy is Key!

We were made to live in God's continual presence, but after the fall that perfect relationship was lost. God desires that we re-establish and enjoy that relationship with Him now. In fact, maintaining a close relationship with God is essential to reigning in life. Our top priority has to be to develop a growing, intimate love relationship with God. He first loved us (1John 4:19) and He longs for us to love Him in return. Our primary identity is derived from being loved by God and then becoming a lover of God. As we enjoy and delight in His loving presence, God delights in us. In this place, we can rest and enjoy simply being who He made us to be.

Here we are truly successful.

God invites us to enjoy friendship and fellowship with all three persons of the Trinity:

May the grace of the Lord Jesus Christ, the love of God, and the fellowship of the Holy Spirit be with you all.
2 Corinthians 13:14

Father: *We proclaim to you what we ourselves have actually seen and heard so that you may have fellowship with us. And our fellowship is with the Father and with his Son, Jesus Christ.*
1 John 1:3

Son: *God will do this, for he is faithful to do what he says, and he has invited you into partnership with his Son, Jesus Christ our Lord.*
1 Corinthians 1:9

Holy Spirit: *And I will ask the Father, and he will give you another Advocate, who will never leave you. He is the Holy Spirit, who leads into all truth. The world cannot receive him, because it isn't looking for him and doesn't recognize him. But you know him, because he lives with you now and later will be in you.*
John 14:16-17

❧

1. How is God's heart for His people expressed in Jeremiah 31:3, Zephaniah 3:17 and 1 John 4:9-10?

"I have loved you, my people, with an everlasting love.
  With unfailing love I have drawn you to myself.
Jeremiah 31:3

For the LORD your God is living among you.
He is a mighty savior.
He will take delight in you with gladness.
With his love, he will calm all your fears.
He will rejoice over you with joyful songs."
Zephaniah 3:17

God showed how much he loved us by sending his one and only Son into the world so that we might have eternal life through him. ¹⁰ This is real love—not that we loved God, but that he loved us and sent his Son as a sacrifice to take away our sins.
1 John 4:9-10

2. Read Ephesians 3:14-19. How does Paul address God as he begins to pray (verses 14-15)? Exactly what does he pray for these believers?

When I think of all this, I fall to my knees and pray to the Father [15] *the Creator of everything in heaven and on earth.* [16] *I pray that from his glorious, unlimited resources he will empower you with inner strength through his Spirit.* [17] *Then Christ will make his home in your hearts as you trust in him. Your roots will grow down into God's love and keep you strong.* [18] *And may you have the power to understand, as all God's people should, how wide, how long, how high, and how deep his love is.* [19] *May you experience the love of Christ, though it is too great to understand fully. Then you will be made complete with all the fullness of life and power that comes from God.*
Ephesians 3:14-19

3. What can you learn about King David's devotion to God expressed in the following Psalms? What practical steps could you take to apply some of these truths to deepen your own relationship with God?

You will show me the way of life,
granting me the joy of your presence
and the pleasures of living with you forever.
Psalm 16:11

Teach me your ways, O LORD,
  that I may live according to your truth!
Grant me purity of heart,
  so that I may honor you.
12 With all my heart I will praise you, O Lord my God.
  I will give glory to your name forever.
Psalm 86:1-3

There's a private place reserved for the lovers of God,
Where they sit near Him and receive
The revelation secrets of His promises.*
Psalm 25:14 (TPT)

*Translator's footnote: Or "covenant." The Hebrew word for "secret" is also the word for "couch." This is the place intimate friends would sit together to talk and to share conversation.

The one thing I ask of the LORD—
  the thing I seek most—
is to live in the house of the LORD all the days of my life,
  delighting in the LORD's perfections
  and meditating in his Temple.
Psalm 27:4

O God, you are my God;
*   I earnestly search for you.*
My soul thirsts for you;
*   my whole body longs for you*
in this parched and weary land
*   where there is no water.*
² I have seen you in your sanctuary
*   and gazed upon your power and glory.*
³ Your unfailing love is better than life itself;
*   how I praise you!*
⁴ I will praise you as long as I live,
*   lifting up my hands to you in prayer.*
⁵ You satisfy me more than the richest feast.
*   I will praise you with songs of joy.*
⁶ I lie awake thinking of you,
*   meditating on you through the night.*
⁷ Because you are my helper,
*   I sing for joy in the shadow of your wings.*
⁸ I cling to you;
*   your strong right hand holds me securely.*
Psalm 63:1-8

Let all that I am praise the LORD;
  with my whole heart, I will praise his holy name.
2 Let all that I am praise the LORD;
  may I never forget the good things he does for me.
3 He forgives all my sins
  and heals all my diseases.
4 He redeems me from death
  and crowns me with love and tender mercies.
5 He fills my life with good things.
  My youth is renewed like the eagle's!
Psalm 103:1-5

4. Our love for God is His gift to us. What does Romans 5:5 tell you about His love?

And this hope is not a disappointing fantasy, because we can now experience the endless love of God cascading into our hearts through the Holy Spirit who lives in us! (TPT)

5. According to 2 Corinthians 3:17-18, how are you changed to become more like the Lord Jesus?

For the Lord is the Spirit, and wherever the Spirit of the Lord is, there is freedom. [18] So all of us who have had that veil removed can see and reflect the glory of the Lord. And the Lord—who is the Spirit—makes us more and more like him as we are changed into his glorious image.

6. In Matthew 11:28-30, what does Jesus offer and to whom? What do you need to do to take advantage of His offer?

Then Jesus said, "Come to me, all of you who are weary and carry heavy burdens, and I will give you rest. [29] Take my yoke upon you. Let me teach you, because I am humble and gentle at heart, and you will find rest for your souls. [30] For my yoke is easy to bear, and the burden I give you is light."

7. What concern did Paul express for the Corinthian Christians in 2 Corinthians 11:3? What can you do to ensure the devil doesn't derail or in any way compromise your intimate love relationship with God?

But I fear that somehow your pure and undivided devotion to Christ will be corrupted, just as Eve was deceived by the cunning ways of the serpent.

"Our greatest satisfaction is to know and feel His love, to love Him and to overflow in love for others. This will have the greatest impact on our heart as our spirit is exhilarated in God's love." ~ Mike Bickle

Suggestion: To deepen your intimacy with God, schedule regular daily "appointments" with Him. Write specific times and locations on your calendar or in your planner, and keep those engagements!

✍

Obedience and Our Love Relationship

It's impossible to love God without seeking to obey His Word. Jesus said in John 14:21, *Those who accept my commandments and obey them are the ones who love me. And because they love me, my Father will love them. And I will love them and reveal myself to each of them.*

Our intimate love relationship with God is never based on Him using us in ministry. We're first lovers and then workers in His Kingdom. We obey Him because we love Him, not to gain His love.

I know there have been times in my life, especially in my early years as a Christian, when I was zealously serving God and I began to equate success in ministry with God's approval and love for me. Obedience then became an obligation rather than a natural response from a heart of love. I found myself trying to earn more of God's love. I didn't fully believe that nothing I did or failed to do could ever cause Him to love me more or less.

⌘

Friendship with God

Jesus expressed His love for the Father in perfect obedience and trust. He beautifully models the obedience required of us as God's friends. Servants and friends have different motivations to obey—servants obey because it's their duty, but friends obey out of love. God wants loving friendship to be the basis of our relationship with Him.

> "The reality is that unless we understand God's heart of love for us and His desire for true, intimate friendship, we won't understand what Jesus is talking about when He says, 'You are my friends if you do whatever I command you' (John 5:14). We will hear that all He cares about is obedience, and that He is telling us to prove our love for Him by doing what He wants. But if we understand what Jesus' relationship with His Father was like, the kind of relationship we've been invited into, we will be able to hear Him saying, 'True obedience is simply the natural response from the heart of a friend, and it's simply doing what I'm doing.'"
> ~ Kris Vallotton, *Basic Training for the Supernatural Ways of Royalty*

Suggestion: Invite the Holy Spirit to give you a deeper revelation of how He feels about you and how He wants you to know Him as a friend. Take some time to talk and interact with Him as you would a dear friend. Ask Him to give you clear understanding of how you can abide in Jesus and let His Word abide in you. Ask Him to show you how to enjoy and rest in Him.

Even the problems and challenges we face can become the subject of a dialogue with Him. We can glean much wisdom in these loving, prayerful conversations. Ask Him questions. For example, "What do You want to teach me through this?" "How do *You* see this situation?" "How should I pray about this?" Listen to Him, and invite His presence in the stillness.

If you use a journal, write the questions you're asking Holy Spirit and the answers He gives you. This will encourage you when you look back later. Use the words you've written for prayer, thanksgiving and praise.

8. What can you learn about Jesus' relationship with the Father from the following scriptures? How does He want you to respond to Him and what will happen as a result?

For I have come down from heaven to do the will of God who sent me, not to do my own will.
John 6:38

[10] Don't you believe that I am in the Father and the Father is in me? The words I speak are not my own, but my Father who lives in me does his work through me.

[23] Jesus replied, "All who love me will do what I say. My Father will love them, and we will come and make our home with each of them.
John 14:10, 23

I have loved you even as the Father has loved me. Remain in my love. [10] When you obey my commandments, you remain in my love, just as I obey my Father's commandments and remain in his love. [11] I have told you these things so that you will be filled with my joy. Yes, your joy will overflow!
John 15:9-11

9. As children of a loving and generous Heavenly Father, how should we approach Him and what should we expect?

"Keep on asking, and you will receive what you ask for. Keep on seeking, and you will find. Keep on knocking, and the door will be opened to you. [8] For everyone who asks, receives. Everyone who seeks, finds. And to everyone who knocks, the door will be opened.

[9] "You parents—if your children ask for a loaf of bread, do you give them a stone instead? [10] Or if they ask for a fish, do you give them a snake? Of course not! [11] So if you sinful people know how to give good gifts to your children, how much more will your heavenly Father give good gifts to those who ask him.
Matthew 7:7-11

Since he did not spare even his own Son but gave him up for us all, won't he also give us everything else?
Romans 8:32

10. Would your relationship with God be different if you trusted and confided in him as you do your best friend? In what ways would it change?

11. What might prevent you from a deep intimacy with God? What might stop you from really believing that He finds you utterly irresistible?

We will inevitably fail and make mistakes in life. When this happens, we must quickly run to our loving heavenly Father, and resist the temptation to turn away from Him because we feel a sense of shame. There before Him we can confess our sin, receive forgiveness and allow His love to flood our hearts again. Failing to do this right away gives the enemy of our souls an opportunity to come and torment us.

When King David was made aware of his sin, he quickly confessed it, repented, asked for and received God's mercy, forgiveness and grace. I'm sure this was one of the secrets to his greatness. Though he did some terrible things, God describes him as, "A man after my own heart," in Acts 13:22.

After committing adultery and murder, King David writes the following in Psalm 51, his prayer of repentance. We can follow his example and even use his words as a guide when we mess up.

Purify my conscience! Make this 'leper' clean again!
Wash me in Your love until I am pure in heart.
Satisfy me in Your sweetness and my song of joy will return.
The places within me You have crushed
Will rejoice in Your healing touch.
Hide my sins from Your face,
Erase all my guilt in Your saving grace.
Start over with me, and create a new, clean heart within me.
Fill me with pure thoughts
And holy desires, ready to please You.
May there never be even a shadow of darkness between us!
May you never deprive me of Your Sacred Spirit!
~ Psalm 51:7-11 (TPT)

∽

"The true, the genuine worship is when man, through his spirit, attains to friendship and intimacy with God. True and genuine worship is not to come to a certain place; it is not to go through a certain ritual or liturgy; it is not even to bring certain gifts. True worship is when the spirit, the immortal and invisible part of man, speaks to and meets with God, who is immortal and invisible." ~ William Barclay

B. Relating to and Honoring Others – Both the Royal Family of God and Those Not yet in the Family

"Royalty is my identity. Servanthood is my assignment. Intimacy with God is my life source." ~ Bill Johnson

The greatest gift we can receive from God is the anointing to experience His love, express it back to Him, and let it flow out onto others.

As royal children of God we are honorable and we are to honor others in the way we relate to them. Remember, those around us in the Body of Christ are royalty too! Instead of seeing them simply with our natural physical eyes or looking at them from the world's viewpoint, we're to see them from God's perspective. They are created in the image of God and are infinitely precious to Him. The price Jesus paid for them on the cross determines their immense value to Him.

It's often easy to see the flaws in other people, but as royal sons and daughters of God, we're called to honor them. We are to look for the "gold" in people rather than focus on their faults. Honor is an attitude of the heart. It releases life in us and in others!

Suggestion: Ask the Holy Spirit to give you a revelation of how He sees and values those around you.

Definition:
Honor: respect that is given to someone who is admired.

12. What can you learn about honor from Jesus' words in Matthew 5:43-48? Is there someone in your life who has not honored you, who has possibly treated you with disrespect? What could you do to show honor to that person as Jesus would?

"You have heard the law that says, 'Love your neighbor' and hate your enemy. [44] But I say, love your enemies! Pray for those who persecute you! [45] In that way, you will be acting as true children of your Father in heaven. For he gives his sunlight to both the evil and the good, and he sends rain on the just and the unjust alike. [46] If you love only those who love you, what reward is there for that? Even corrupt tax collectors do that much. [47] If you are kind only to your friends, how are you different from anyone else? Even pagans do that. [48] But you are to be perfect, even as your Father in heaven is perfect.

13. On what occasions in your life have you felt the most honored? The least honored?

14. How easy or difficult is it for you to receive honor from others? Why?

15. In John 13:1-17, how did Jesus honor his disciples? Why did He do this? What did He want the disciples to learn from this? How can you apply this teaching in a practical way to honor those you interact with daily?

"We are to rule with the heart of a servant and serve with the heart of a king."
~ Bill Johnson

16. What individuals and/or groups of people in your sphere of influence could you honor in a special way? Who will you speak words of life and encouragement to today?

17. What practical steps can you take to increase honor in your home and/or work environment?

18. In Romans 15:7 and 12:9-10, what does Paul direct his readers to do that would honor others? Are there people you find difficult to accept? What could you do to more fully accept and honor them?

Therefore, accept each other just as Christ has accepted you so that God will be given glory.
Romans 15:7

Don't just pretend to love others. Really love them. Hate what is wrong. Hold tightly to what is good. ¹⁰ Love each other with genuine affection, and take delight in honoring each other.
Romans 12:9-10

19. What does Colossians 3:12-14 say about honoring others? How do you think you can 'put on' or 'clothe yourself' with love? When you do this, what does Paul say the result will be?

Since God chose you to be the holy people he loves, you must clothe yourselves with tender-hearted mercy, kindness, humility, gentleness, and patience. ¹³ Make allowance for each other's faults, and forgive anyone who offends you. Remember, the Lord forgave you, so you must forgive others. ¹⁴ Above all, clothe yourselves with love, which binds us all together in perfect harmony.
Colossians 3:12-14

20. In Philippians 2:1-11, Paul tells his readers what would make him truly happy. What is it? What should they do? Not do? How does this relate to honoring others? How might Jesus' example described in verses 6-11 motivate you to do the same?

Is there any encouragement from belonging to Christ? Any comfort from his love? Any fellowship together in the Spirit? Are your hearts tender and compassionate? ² *Then make me truly happy by agreeing wholeheartedly with each other, loving one another, and working together with one mind and purpose.*

³ *Don't be selfish; don't try to impress others. Be humble, thinking of others as better than yourselves.* ⁴ *Don't look out only for your own interests, but take an interest in others, too.*

⁵ *You must have the same attitude that Christ Jesus had.*

⁶ *Though he was God,*
  he did not think of equality with God
  as something to cling to.
⁷ *Instead, he gave up his divine privileges;*
  he took the humble position of a slave
  and was born as a human being.
When he appeared in human form,
⁸ *he humbled himself in obedience to God*
  and died a criminal's death on a cross.

⁹ *Therefore, God elevated him to the place of highest honor*
  and gave him the name above all other names,
¹⁰ *that at the name of Jesus every knee should bow,*
  in heaven and on earth and under the earth,
¹¹ *and every tongue declare that Jesus Christ is Lord,*
  to the glory of God the Father.
Philippians 2:1-11

21. What assignment does Paul give his readers in 2 Corinthians 5:18-21? How would they need to honor others—those not yet in the royal family—in order to fulfill this role? How does this apply to you today?

And all of this is a gift from God, who brought us back to himself through Christ. And God has given us this task of reconciling people to him. ¹⁹ For God was in Christ, reconciling the world to himself, no longer counting people's sins against them. And he gave us this wonderful message of reconciliation. ²⁰ So we are Christ's ambassadors; God is making his appeal through us. We speak for Christ when we plead, "Come back to God!" ²¹ For God made Christ, who never sinned, to be the offering for our sin, so that we could be made right with God through Christ.
2 Corinthians 5:18-21

22. Prayerfully make a list of those whom you find difficult to love and honor. Ask God to help you through the power of His Holy Spirit to see them with His eyes, to love and honor them, and to give you opportunities to express this love.

The next and final study in this series is *Pursue Your Divine Destiny*. In it you'll explore how to position yourself to discover, follow and keep on track to fulfill God's destiny for your life.

> "And he has given you a destiny — *something to do in this life,*
> *something only you can do*. Before you were born, God wired you with
> certain ambitions, desires, and drives to play a particular role in history
> — one that only you can play." ~ Rick Warren

Prayer Requests and Notes

_____

_____

_____

_____

_____

_____

_____

_____

_____

_____

_____

_____

_____

_____

_____

_____

_____

_____

_____

Study Six
Pursue Your Divine Destiny

A. Discover Your Destiny

"Jesus made us a kingdom, priests to God. That's a quotation of Exodus 19:6. 'Ye shall be unto me a kingdom of priests, and a holy nation.' He has given us royalty. Through Him we may become true sons of God; and, if we are sons of the King of kings, then we are of lineage which there can be none more royal. Our destiny is a royal destiny." ~ William Barclay

"There is no greater discovery than seeing God as the author of your destiny." ~ Ravi Zacharias

Declarations:

- I have a royal destiny and I am pursing it! (Revelation 1:6)

- I abide in Christ and listen to His voice. (John 15:5 and 16:13)

- God has creative solutions to help me achieve my destiny. (Ephesians 3:20)

God has put within each of us a desire to be successful—to be great for Him! He created us to dream, to plan, to want to be remarkable and to accomplish amazing things for Him. Desiring these things is natural and not necessarily prideful.

We are designed to be successful, but need a biblical understanding of what that means. How our humanistic culture defines success is very different from God's view of success. People around us think of success as financial and material wealth, fame and prestige. In God's eyes, a successful person is someone who is surrendered to Him and committed to love. It is someone who willingly trusts and obeys, regardless of any opposition or cost.

> "More than other idols, personal success and achievement lead to a sense that we ourselves are God, that our security and value rest in our own wisdom, strength and performance. To be the very best at what you do, to be at the top of the heap, means no one is like you. You are supreme."
> ~ Tim Keller, *Counterfeit Gods*

In His prayer to the Father in John 17, Jesus said, *I have glorified You on the earth. I have finished the work which You have given Me to do.* He did what He came to do. He achieved His destiny and, as His followers, we are to seek and fulfill our divine destiny on earth. When seeking God for our destiny, it's important that we keep in mind our true identity as royal sons or daughters of the King. Our Father knows everything about us—all we've ever done, said and thought. He knows our gifts, the dreams and aspirations in our hearts, our strengths and weaknesses, doubts and fears—everything! He is extravagantly loving and generous, desires the absolute best for every one of His sons and daughters, and has prepared a unique plan—a divine destiny—for each one of us. He has set us up for success!

We have a natural desire to know God's will for our lives. He wants us to find and follow the future He's planned for us, but He wants our hearts even more. He desires an increasingly close friendship with us every step of the way. Without this relationship, we will never be able to reach our destiny.

> "Many people want to know the will of God for their lives. But I'm not sure we can know or understand this unless our hearts respond to Him in love. This is more important to God than anything we can do for Him. Jesus is after our hearts. He will use whatever it takes to awaken us to receive and respond to His love. He is love and everything He does is for love." ~ Mike Bickle

Note: In seeking your God-given destiny, keep in mind that there is no distinction between "secular" and "sacred." All God's callings are sacred!

1. What can you discover about God's plan for your life from the following verses?

You watched me as I was being formed in utter seclusion,
    as I was woven together in the dark of the womb.
16 You saw me before I was born.
    Every day of my life was recorded in your book.
Every moment was laid out
    before a single day had passed.
Psalm 139:15-16

We have become His poetry,* a recreated people that will fulfill the destiny He has given each
of us, for we are joined to Jesus, the Anointed One. Even before we were born, God planned in
advance our destiny and the good works we would do to fulfill it!
Ephesians 2:10 (TPT)

*Translator's note: "The beautiful Greek word used here is translated 'poem' or 'poetry.' Our lives are the beautiful poetry written by God that will speak forth all that He desires in life."

So be careful how you live. Don't live like fools, but like those who are wise. [16] Make the most of every opportunity in these evil days. [17] Don't act thoughtlessly, but understand what the Lord wants you to do.
Ephesians 5:15-17

And I am certain that God, who began the good work within you, will continue his work until it is finally finished on the day when Christ Jesus returns.
Philippians 1:6

2. In Romans 12:1-2, what does Paul say is an appropriate response to God's mercies? What do these verses say you should do? Not do? How do the truths here relate to your destiny?

Beloved friends, what should be our proper response to God's marvelous mercies? I encourage you to surrender yourselves to God to be his sacred, living sacrifices. And live in holiness, experiencing all that delights his heart. For this becomes your genuine expression of worship.

[2] Stop imitating the ideals and opinions of the culture around you, but be inwardly transformed by the Holy Spirit through a total reformation of how you think. This will empower you to discern God's will as you live a beautiful life, satisfying and perfect in his eyes.
Romans 12:1-2 (TPT)

3. Although God's promises in Jeremiah 29:11-13 were given to the people of Israel, these truths are valid for us today. How can you apply these promises in your life? What condition does God require?

For I know the plans I have for you," says the LORD. "They are plans for good and not for disaster, to give you a future and a hope. ¹² In those days when you pray, I will listen. ¹³ If you look for me wholeheartedly, you will find me.

"Jesus has prepared the way and has made following our destiny possible, whereas we are helpless by ourselves. We can find and fulfill our purpose by responding to the clear, simple call of Jesus Christ: 'Follow Me.' He is the doorway to fulfilling our destiny, where our divine design and God-ordained purpose live in perfect harmony." ~ Charles R. Swindoll

4. Ask God how He sees your future, and what you can do now to prepare for it. Write below what you sense He is saying to you, and also record any promises and/or scriptures He has given you in the past.

5. According to the following scriptures, how may God guide you? What can you do to hear the His voice more clearly? What might prevent this?

The LORD says, "I will guide you along the best pathway for your life.
  I will advise you and watch over you.
⁹ Do not be like a senseless horse or mule
  that needs a bit and bridle to keep it under control."
Psalm 32:8-9

Yet I still belong to you;
    you hold my right hand.
[24] *You guide me with your counsel,*
    leading me to a glorious destiny.
Psalm 73:23-24

Trust in the LORD with all your heart;
    do not depend on your own understanding.
[6] *Seek his will in all you do,*
    and he will show you which path to take.
Proverbs 3:5-6

We can make our plans,
  but the LORD determines our steps.
Proverbs 16:9

When the Spirit of truth comes, he will guide you into all truth. He will not speak on his own but will tell you what he has heard. He will tell you about the future.
John 16:13

For all who are led by the Spirit of God are children of God.
[15] So you have not received a spirit that makes you fearful slaves. Instead, you received God's Spirit when he adopted you as his own children. Now we call him, "Abba, Father."
Romans 8:14-15

"Finding and fulfilling your purpose is the greatest adventure you can have in this life, and should be a top priority for every Christian." ~ Rick Joyner

6. An important factor in discovering your destiny is to seek input from godly advisors. Find a few wise and trustworthy counselors who believe in you and whom you know will be objective, listen carefully, and answer slowly. Ask the Father who would best fill this mentoring role in your life. When He answers, approach this person with your request.

   According to Proverbs 11:14 and 15:22 what potential benefits can be gained from this?

Without wise leadership, a nation falls;
   there is safety in having many advisers.
Proverbs 11:14

Plans go wrong for lack of advice;
   many advisers bring success.
Proverbs 15:22

If you solicit good advice, then your plans will succeed!
So don't charge into battle without wisdom,
For wars are won by skillful strategy.
Proverbs 20:18 (TPT)

7. Prayerfully read 1 Peter 4:10-11 and Romans 12:6-8. What gifts listed in these passages (and maybe other gifts not included here) do you feel God has given you? How have you used these gifts to date? How would you like to see yourself using these gifts to serve others in future?

God has given each of you a gift from his great variety of spiritual gifts. Use them well to serve one another. [11] Do you have the gift of speaking? Then speak as though God himself were speaking through you. Do you have the gift of helping others? Do it with all the strength and energy that God supplies. Then everything you do will bring glory to God through Jesus Christ. All glory and power to him forever and ever! Amen.
1 Peter 4:10-11

In his grace, God has given us different gifts for doing certain things well. So if God has given you the ability to prophesy, speak out with as much faith as God has given you. [7] If your gift is serving others, serve them well. If you are a teacher, teach well. [8] If your gift is to encourage others, be encouraging. If it is giving, give generously. If God has given you leadership ability, take the responsibility seriously. And if you have a gift for showing kindness to others, do it gladly.
Romans 12:6-8

Suggestion: You may want to seek local opportunities, even small ones, as part of your training in order to find out how it feels to use your gifts in this way.

8. Write down, review and talk to the Holy Spirit about any prophetic words you've been given. Ask Him to show you how any of these words may relate to your destiny. Write below what He shows you.

"God's looking for people through whom He can do the impossible. What a pity that we plan only things we can do by ourselves." ~ A.W. Tozer

Questions to Ask Yourself:

9. What are you passionate about? What do you really enjoy doing? What do you feel strongly about that is really important to you?

10. What thoughts or dreams about your future keep coming to mind?

"Simply knowing what your destiny is doesn't guarantee you'll achieve it. It will take dedication and commitment on your part to follow through and get to where God has designed and destined you to be." ~ Gregory Giagnocavo

11. In what areas of your life have you been successful and seen fruit in the past?

A tree is identified by its fruit. If a tree is good, its fruit will be good. If a tree is bad, its fruit will be bad.
Matthew 12:33

"If you're not overwhelmed by your assignment, then you don't see your assignment clearly." ~ Bill Johnson

Note: God may call you to do something for which you have no natural gifting or background. For example, Paul was a zealous, well educated religious Jew, but God called him to be an Apostle to the Gentiles. While Peter, an uneducated fisherman, became leader of the church in Jerusalem composed mainly of religious Jews.

12. God may ask you to do something way beyond your comfort zone. It may be something that appears foolish in the world's eyes, even something no one has done to date. How will you feel about this? What might hold you back from wholeheartedly pursuing it? What would encourage you to move ahead by faith trusting God?

13. You probably won't achieve your dreams overnight and it may not be easy or work out just the way you expected. Joseph waited many years before the dreams God gave him came to fruition. From Psalm 105:16-23 and Genesis 39:1 through 41:57, what do you think Joseph learned from God during this time? What can you learn from his example?

We can't afford to spend any energy thinking about what we don't have, who we're not or how hard and impossible it will be to succeed. We must keep our eyes on Jesus, His unshakable love for us, and the promises He's given us. We must pray with God's promises and purposes in mind, and not in line with our problems. When we doubt, we are helping the enemy with his goal to make us unsuccessful.

As you think about your future, how God has equipped you and is leading you, seek to maintain an attitude of thankfulness. Beware of comparing yourself, your gifting, and the opportunities God has given you with others and their gifts, etc.

> "Currently, there are seven billion people on earth. Each one is unique, different by design. God doesn't need you to 'be' anyone else. He designed you, to be you. If you covet what someone else is or talents they have, you are insulting God who created you." ~ Gregory Giagnocavo

B. Overcome Obstacles Along the Way

God desires that we become increasingly like Jesus in how we perceive, think, speak and act. He will use all the circumstances, setbacks, and successes we meet along the way to that end.

He has already planned our future—our destiny. We are simply to partner with Him as we step out and follow His plan. However, the devil is often more aware of our God-given gifting and assignments than we are, and will likely try to discourage and intimidate us in those very areas we are to influence for God. We must stay alert and not allow him to sidetrack us from what God has called us to do.

> "God never reminds us of our smallness when He calls us to do something awesome. Instead He calls us to courage by proclaiming something amazing over us like, 'You're a mighty warrior,' 'A father of many nations,' or 'You're the one that all of Israel is waiting on!'" ~ Kris Vallotton

14. God has creative solutions for every obstacle we will ever face. Are you currently facing a problem or is there something you think may prevent you from reaching your destiny? Meditate on Ephesians 3:20, then ask God to show you how He sees the situation and what He wants you to do about it. Write what He shows you and the solutions He gives you below.

Now to Him Who, by (in consequence of) the [action of His] power that is at work within us, is able to [carry out His purpose and] do superabundantly, far over and above all that we [dare] ask or think [infinitely beyond our highest prayers, desires, thoughts, hopes, or dreams]— (AMPCE)

15. At times you will face setbacks and challenges. How can you prepare for this and guard your heart from discouragement, disillusionment, and/or doubt?

16. Ask the Holy Spirit to show you any lies are you believe that may prevent you from reaching your destiny? White them below, along with the opposite truths.

17. How can you stay more focused on your destiny so that you will be able to say with the Apostle Paul at the end of your life, *I have fought the good fight, I have finished the race, and I have remained faithful.* ~ 2 Timothy 4:7? What must you do now to keep energized as you pursue your divine destiny?

Confront Regret

In any study on destiny, the memory of past failures and consequent regret is almost inevitable. We've all made mistakes, missed opportunities and done and said things we wish we hadn't. We can learn valuable lessons from our mistakes, but need to be careful not to dwell on these in a way that allows the enemy to use them to discourage or disable us.

Several recent secular studies show that at the end of their lives people are most likely to regret the things they failed to do.

> "Of all sad words of tongue or pen,
> the saddest are, 'It might have been.'"
> ~ John Greenleaf Whittier

18. What can you learn about overcoming regret from Peter's example in the following scriptures? How did he deal with his regret?

"But why can't I come now, Lord?" he asked. "I'm ready to die for you."

[38] *Jesus answered, "Die for me? I tell you the truth, Peter—before the rooster crows tomorrow morning, you will deny three times that you even know me.*
John 13:37-38

Meanwhile, Peter was sitting outside in the courtyard. A servant girl came over and said to him, "You were one of those with Jesus the Galilean."

[70] *But Peter denied it in front of everyone. "I don't know what you're talking about," he said.*

[71] *Later, out by the gate, another servant girl noticed him and said to those standing around, "This man was with Jesus of Nazareth."*

[72] *Again Peter denied it, this time with an oath. "I don't even know the man," he said.*

[73] *A little later some of the other bystanders came over to Peter and said, "You must be one of them; we can tell by your Galilean accent."*

[74] *Peter swore, "A curse on me if I'm lying—I don't know the man!" And immediately the rooster crowed.*

[75] Suddenly, Jesus' words flashed through Peter's mind: "Before the rooster crows, you will deny three times that you even know me." And he went away, weeping bitterly.
Matthew 26:69-75

From the verses below, how did Jesus encourage him?

Now go and tell his disciples, including Peter, that Jesus is going ahead of you to Galilee. You will see him there, just as he told you before he died.
Mark 16:7

A third time he asked him, "Simon son of John, do you love me?"

Peter was hurt that Jesus asked the question a third time. He said, "Lord, you know everything. You know that I love you."

Jesus said, "Then feed my sheep."
John 21:17

What was the result in Acts 2:40-41 and Acts 9:32-43?

Then Peter continued preaching for a long time, strongly urging all his listeners, "Save yourselves from this crooked generation!"

⁴¹ Those who believed what Peter said were baptized and added to the church that day—about 3,000 in all.
Acts 2:40-41

19. Read Galatians 1:13-16 and Philippians 3:13-14. How did Paul deal with regret? What can you learn from this that could be helpful to you in the future?

You know what I was like when I followed the Jewish religion—how I violently persecuted God's church. I did my best to destroy it. ¹⁴ I was far ahead of my fellow Jews in my zeal for the traditions of my ancestors.

¹⁵ But even before I was born, God chose me and called me by his marvelous grace. Then it pleased him ¹⁶ to reveal his Son to me so that I would proclaim the Good News about Jesus to the Gentiles.
Galatians 1:13-16

No, dear brothers and sisters, I have not achieved it, but I focus on this one thing: Forgetting the past and looking forward to what lies ahead, ¹⁴ I press on to reach the end of the race and receive the heavenly prize for which God, through Christ Jesus, is calling us.
Philippians 3:13-14

20. How can Romans 8:1 encourage you when you think of past failures and mistakes?

So now there is no condemnation for those who belong to Christ Jesus.

"Set goals so big that unless God helps you, you will be a miserable failure."
~ Bill Bright, *The Journey Home: Finishing with Joy*

21. Write your "Destiny Declaration" – a short paragraph about God's vision for your life in the future—your divine destiny.

"Only one life, 'twill soon be past,
Only what's done for Christ will last."
~ C.T. Studd

❧

"*And there will be no night there—no need for lamps or sun—for the Lord God will shine on them. **And they will reign forever and ever.***"
Revelation 22:5 (Emphasis added)

Prayer Requests and Notes

_____

_____

_____

_____

_____

_____

_____

_____

_____

_____

_____

_____

_____

_____

_____

_____

_____

_____

_____

_____

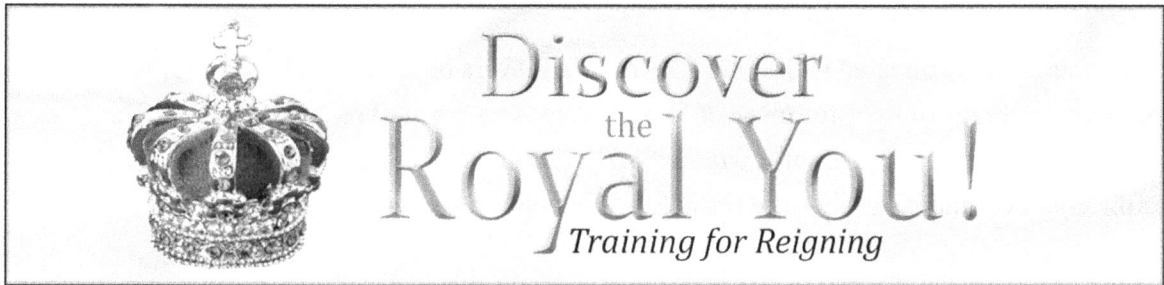

What Now?

My Desire for You, the Reader:

I pray you will see yourself more and more as the royal son or daughter of God you truly are. I'm asking the Holy Spirit to remind you to think, act and speak in a way that's fitting for a royal son or daughter. May you see your circumstances increasingly the way God sees them—from above—where you're seated with Christ in the heavenly realms.

I suggest you ask God to continually alert you to any lies you're tempted to believe, so that you can deal with them promptly and focus on the opposite truth. Step out in faith and be bold to use your royal, God-given authority whenever it's appropriate.

Look back from time to time at what you wrote in your studies, especially at any changes you planned to make. If the Holy Spirit shows you areas of your life that need to be changed or tuned up, ask Him to show you how to do this and to give you the grace* to follow through faithfully. Review and renew commitments if necessary and allow God's powerful Word to transform your life.

Plan to take time daily with God—talk to Him, listen to Him and read your Bible, asking Him to make it alive and relevant as you do. Getting to know ever more deeply the God who created and sustains everything, who knows you intimately, loves you passionately, and totally delights in you, *will* change your life! You will gain a deeper understanding of yourself, your God-given destiny, and how to achieve it as you partner with God.

The Christian life isn't easy! We're in a war with no cease-fire in sight. We seriously need one another and plenty of support and encouragement along the way. So be sure to find a good

*A definition of *grace*: God's supernatural empowering and enabling presence.

church and stay connected with other like-minded lovers of Jesus. Ask God to bring friends to you who are really hungry for more of Him, and make a point of reaching out and encouraging others. Perhaps find a mentor who will help you and hold you accountable. Press on to know God ever more deeply—the rewards are beyond measure!

It's my prayer that at the end of our lives, we'll all to be able to say with the Apostle Paul,

> *I have fought the good fight, I have finished the race, and I have remained faithful.* [8] *And now the prize awaits me—the crown of righteousness, which the Lord, the righteous Judge, will give me on the day of his return. And the prize is not just for me but for all who eagerly look forward to his appearing.*
> 2 Timothy 4:7-8

Though I've written Bible studies for decades, this study series has been the most challenging. While writing it, I sensed greater resistance than I've experienced before. Possibly because the truths covered in these studies are so crucial for all who long to live fully for the King of kings at this time in history.

I wrote this study series because I wanted to learn more about my true identity in Christ and how to live life more fully as God designed and intended me to live. How we see ourselves and how we believe God sees us dramatically affects our relationship with Him and with others. It determines how we live and how God is able to use us.

I'd love to hear from you. Please let me know how these studies have impacted your life.

> "To be a son or daughter of God also means you are royalty. This is the greatest of privileges, but it is also an awesome responsibility. If you are truly thankful to God and want to please Him with all your heart, you must do more than just recognize your own authority. You must use it. He asks you to give love as freely as you have received it — not just to those who deserve it but also to everyone He puts in front of you."
> ~ Heidi Baker, *Birthing the Miraculous*

Discover the Royal You! Training for Reigning

Endnotes

Quotation Authors

Neil T. Anderson

Neil Anderson is founder and president of Freedom in Christ Ministries (FICM). He was formerly Professor of Practical Theology at Talbot School of Theology in La Mirada, California. While there, he became aware of his students' needs to connect with God in a more intimate way. As a result, he began teaching a graduate level course, "Resolving Personal and Spiritual Conflicts." He has since been teaching a message on identity, position, authority, and victory in Christ to churches in the U.S. and around the world. Dr. Anderson has authored several bestselling books on spiritual freedom.

www.ficm.org

Thomas Aquinas
1225-1274

Thomas Aquinas was a Catholic priest of the Dominican Order, and a noted philosopher and theologian. His philosophy and teaching strongly influenced Western thought and Christian theology, especially in the Roman Catholic Church.

Augustine of Hippo
(Aurelius Augustinus)
354-430

Augustine of Hippo, often referred to as simply "Augustine," was a philosopher and theologian whose writings influenced Western Christianity and philosophy. He framed the concept of original sin and just war. He was the Bishop of Hippo Regius (modern-day Annaba, Algeria). Augustine was one of the most prolific Latin authors in terms of surviving works, which consists of more than a hundred separate titles.

William Barclay

1907-1978

William Barclay was a theologian, Greek scholar, and author, as well as a radio and television presenter. He was also a Church of Scotland minister, a Professor of Divinity and Biblical Criticism at the University of Glasgow, and a life-long student himself. While too liberal and modern for much of the church, his scholarly and astute commentaries on Scripture are enlightening and deeply enriching. The 17 volumes of the set were all best-sellers and still are to this day. Barclay wrote many other popular books, always drawing on scholarship, but written in a highly accessible style.

Heidi Baker

Heidi Baker and her husband, Rolland, are Christian missionaries and itinerant speakers. Heidi is also the CEO of Iris Global (previously Iris Ministries), a Christian humanitarian organization based in Mozambique, Africa. Iris Global's operations now include well-drilling, free health clinics, village feeding programs, operation of primary and secondary schools and cottage industries. More than 5,000 churches have been founded by them in Mozambique, in addition to a total of over 10,000 Iris-affiliated churches in more than 20 nations. Numerous miracles have been reported in their ministry.

Heidi and Rolland live in Pemba, Mozambique. In addition to their administrative duties, they are active authors and frequent conference speakers.

www.irisglobal.org

Mike Bickle

Mike Bickle is an American evangelical Christian leader best known as director of the International House of Prayer (IHOP) in Kansas City, MO. IHOPKC is an evangelical missions organization based on 24/7 prayer and worship. They plant houses of prayer, train missionaries and engage with many evangelistic and inner-city outreaches and justice initiatives. Their uninterrupted worship and team led non-stop prayer have continued since 1999.

Mike's teaching emphasizes growing in passion for Jesus through intimacy with God, evangelism, missions work, and the end times. He also has authored several books.

www.mikebickle.org

Henry T. Blackaby

Henry Blackaby is a minister and author of the popular Bible study, *Experiencing God*. He has served as a music director, education director, and pastor in churches in California and in Canada. He also served as president of Canadian Baptist Theological College and as president of the Canadian Southern Baptist Conference.

The heart-cry of his ministry is to help people to experience God. He does this through extensive writing, speaking, and teaching.

www.blackaby.net

Bill Bright
1921 –2003

Bill Bright was an American evangelist who, with his wife Vonette, started Campus Crusade for Christ (now known in the United States as Cru) in 1951. They spent more than half a century building and leading Cru to its current size of more than 27,000 staff members and 225,000 volunteers working in 190 countries.

In 1996 Bill Bright was awarded the $1.1 million Templeton Prize for Progress in Religion, and donated the money to promote the spiritual benefits of fasting and prayer.

He authored more than 100 books and booklets, including *Four Spiritual Laws*—a four-point outline on how to establish a personal relationship with Jesus Christ—which has been printed in some 200 languages.

www.cru.org

Graham Cooke

Originally from Manchester, England, Graham Cooke is a popular speaker with a passion to empower God's people to walk in their true identity. He is a commanding communicator with a radiant awareness of Jesus and the Kingdom of God. His life and ministry are marked by his delightful, intimate, and unreserved friendship with the Lord.

Graham now lives in California, and is a consultant to numerous churches, organizations, and businesses. His prophetic insights are much sought after by a variety of organizations around the world. He has authored and published many books.

www.brilliantperspectives.com

Gloria Copeland

Gloria Copeland and her husband, Kenneth, understand just how life-changing the message of faith can be. They have trusted God, based their lives on His Word and have experienced His blessing. Through their ministry they now help thousands of others to do the same.

www.kcm.org/about-us

Francis Frangipane

Francis Frangipane is a Christian evangelical minister and author. He was the founding pastor of River of Life Ministries in Cedar Rapids, Iowa. He has traveled throughout the world ministering to thousands of pastors and intercessors from many backgrounds.
He also has an active partnership with the Mission America Coalition, consisting of leaders from 81 denominations and over 400 ministries and networks. He is a popular teacher in various charismatic and evangelical church settings, in both black and white communities. He now devotes himself to prayer and the ministry of God's Word.

Francis has written several books, including four which were developed for his online school, plus a number of study booklets.

www.frangipane.org

Gregory Giagnocavo

In 1998, Gregory and his wife Anita, moved from Pennsylvania to Guatemala. Together they established Hands of Hope, a medical mission, providing health care to approximately 10,000 impoverished villagers.

Gregory, an entrepreneur and businessman with a technology focus, uses business as a vehicle to take the Gospel to other nations. He is also an international speaker who is always searching for new ways to take the love of Jesus to a lost and dying world.

www.facebook.com/Hands-of-Hope-Medical-Mission

Bill Johnson

Bill and his wife, Beni, are the senior pastors of Bethel Church in Redding, California. Bill is a fifth generation pastor with a rich spiritual heritage. Together they serve a growing number of churches that have partnered for revival. This apostolic network has crossed denominational lines, building relationships that enable church leaders to walk in purity and power.

When they started to minister at Bethel, the outpouring of the Holy Spirit began almost immediately, although in seed form. It grew rapidly and they began to see many healings, including multiple cases of cancer. Healings and miracles have become normal at Bethel today and they rejoice in this!

Bill is also a prolific author.

www.bjm.org (Bill Johnson Ministries)

Rick Joyner

Rick Joyner is founder and Executive Director of MorningStar Ministries, Heritage International Ministries, and is the founder, executive director, and senior pastor of MorningStar Fellowship Church in Fort Mill, South Carolina. He is also president of The Oak Initiative, an interdenominational movement that mobilizes Christians to engage in the principal issues of our time.

Rick is also a well-known author of more than thirty books.

www.morningstarministries.org

Timothy Keller

Dr. Keller is an American pastor, theologian and Christian apologist. He is best known as the founding pastor of Redeemer Presbyterian Church in Manhattan, which he started in 1989 with his wife, Kathy. His diverse congregation of young professionals has grown to a weekly attendance of over 5,000.

He is also chairman of Redeemer City to City, which starts new churches in New York and other cities, and publishes books and resources for faith in urban cultures. He has also authored several New York Times bestselling books.

www.timothykeller.com

Kathryn Kuhlman
1907–1976

Kathryn Kuhlman was an American healing evangelist who traveled extensively in the United States and other countries, holding healing crusades between 1940 and 1970. In 1965, Kathryn focused most of her efforts on Los Angeles where she conducted regular services in the 7,000-seat Shrine Auditorium. She also co-authored a series of books with Jamie Buckingham.

www.kathrynkuhlman.com

C.S. Lewis
1898-1963

C.S. Lewis was a prolific Irish writer and scholar, best known for his fantasy series *The Chronicles of Narnia* and his other Christian books.

Lewis graduated from Oxford University with a focus on literature and classic philosophy. He was awarded a fellowship teaching position at Magdalen College, Oxford University. During that time, he also joined The Inklings, an informal group of writers and intellectuals which included J.R.R. Tolkien. Through conversations with this group Lewis found himself re-embracing Christianity after having become disillusioned with the faith as a youth. The books he authored won many awards.

www.cslewis.com/us

Joyce Meyer

Joyce Meyer is a charismatic Christian author and speaker. Through Joyce Meyer Ministries, she teaches on a number of topics with a particular focus on the mind, mouth, moods, and attitudes. Through her candid and very practical communication style, she shares openly about her experiences so others can apply what she has learned.

Her television and radio programs air in 25 languages in 200 countries. She has authored nearly 100 books, which have been translated into 100 languages. In 2005, *Time Magazine's* "25 Most Influential Evangelicals in America" ranked Joyce Meyer as number 17.

www.joycemeyer.org

Watchman Nee
1903-1972

Watchman Nee was a Chinese Christian author and church leader. Together with others, he founded the Church Assembly Hall, which later became known as "local churches."

Watchman Nee became a Christian at age 17 and began writing the same year. He attended no theological schools or Bible institutes. His knowledge was acquired through Bible study and reading various Christian books. During his 30 years of ministry, he traveled throughout China planting churches in rural communities and holding Christian conferences and training seminars in Shanghai. He was severely persecuted by the Communists and in 1952 was imprisoned for his faith. He remained in prison for the next 20 years until his death.

www.watchmannee.org

Henri J.M. Nouwen
1932-1996

Henri Nouwen was born in Holland and ordained a Catholic priest. He obtained his doctorandus in psychology from Nijmegen University in The Netherlands. He experienced the monastic life with Trappist monks at the Abbey of the Genesee, and lived among the poor in Latin America with the Maryknoll missioners.

After nearly two decades of teaching at academic institutions, including the University of Notre Dame, Yale Divinity School, and Harvard Divinity School, Nouwen went on to work with mentally and physically handicapped people at the L'Arche Daybreak community in Richmond Hill, Ontario.

He wrote over 40 books that have sold millions of copies and have been translated into dozens of languages.

www.henrinouwen.org

Arthur W. Pink

1865-1952

Born in Nottingham, England, Arthur Pink was a Christian evangelist, influential evangelical author, and biblical scholar known for his staunchly Calvinist and Puritan-like teachings.

Desiring to grow in his knowledge of the Bible, he immigrated to the United States to study at Moody Bible Institute. However, after just two months he left for Colorado and later moved to California before returning to Britain. He pastored United States churches in Colorado, California, Kentucky, and South Carolina. He also pastored in Australia.

John Piper

John Piper is a Reformed and Baptist theologian, preacher, and author. He completed a Master of Divinity degree at Fuller Theological Seminary in Pasadena, California; then did doctoral work in New Testament Studies at the University of Munich in Germany.

Sensing an irresistible call to preach in 1980, he became the senior pastor of Bethlehem Baptist Church in Minneapolis, Minnesota, where he ministered for 33 years. He is dedicated to spreading a passion for the supremacy of God in all things, and for the joy of all peoples through Jesus Christ—a mission he continues for the wider church through the ministry of DesiringGod.org.

John has authored over 50 books. He writes regularly and frequently travels to speak.

http://www.desiringgod.org

Alan Redpath

1907-1989

Alan Redpath was a well-known British evangelist, pastor, and author. He was pastor of Duke Street Baptist Church in Richmond, London. In 1953, he moved to the United States and became the pastor of the Moody Church in Chicago.

Returning to the United Kingdom in 1962, he became pastor of Charlotte Baptist Chapel, Edinburgh, Scotland, where he suffered and then recovered from a near-fatal stroke. He became Field Representative for Capernwray Missionary Fellowship, and later was named Pastoral Dean of Capernwray Bible School. He also authored several books.

Charles H. Spurgeon

1834-1892

Charles Haddon Spurgeon was an English Baptist pastor and writer, known as the "Prince of Preachers." He was converted to Christ at the age of 16 and immediately began preaching. Initially, he preached on the streets and in the fields. His first church started with 100 members and grew until he was preaching to 10,000. His boyish appearance contrasted sharply with the maturity of his sermons. His church, the Metropolitan Tabernacle, seated 6,000 people. His preaching was both enormously popular and highly controversial.

Although Spurgeon had no formal education beyond Newmarket Academy (a local community school), he was very well-read in Puritan theology, natural history, Latin and Victorian literature. His lack of a college degree was no hindrance to his remarkable preaching career. He published more than 2,000 sermons and 49 volumes of commentaries, anccdotcs, illustrations, and dcvotions.

www.spurgeon.org

John Stott

1921 - 2011

John Stott was an evangelical Anglican minister and teacher of Scripture. Ordained in 1945, he became a curate and then rector of All Souls Church, Langham Place, London. He grew up and spent most of his life in this church, aside from the time he studied at Trinity College Cambridge.

He was a leader among evangelicals in Britain, the United States, and around the world, and is famous as one of the principal authors of the Lausanne Covenant in 1974.

In April 2005, he was listed in *Time Magazine's* "100 Most Influential People" and was named in the Queen's New Years Honors list as Commander of the Order of the British Empire (CBE) on December 31, 2005.

www.johnstottmemorial.org

C.T. Studd

1860–1931

Charles Thomas Studd, often known as C.T. Studd, was a well-known British cricketer and missionary. As a missionary to China, he was part of the famous "Cambridge Seven."

From 1900-1906, Studd was pastor of a church in South India. Although this was very different from the pioneering missionary work in China, his ministry there was marked by numerous conversions amongst the British officials and the local community. On his return home, he became concerned about large parts of Africa that had never been reached with the Gospel, and in 1910 he went to the Sudan. He set up Heart of Africa Mission which became the Worldwide Evangelisation Crusade (now WEC International). When challenged as to why he was preparing for a life of inevitable hardship in Africa, he replied, "If Jesus Christ be God and died for me, then no sacrifice can be too great for me to make for Him."

Charles R. Swindoll

Charles Swindoll is an evangelical Christian pastor, educator, and radio preacher. He has devoted his life to the accurate, practical teaching, and application of God's Word and His grace. He has served as senior pastor to congregations in Texas, Massachusetts, and California. Since 1998, Chuck has served as the founder and senior pastor-teacher of Stonebriar Community Church in Frisco, Texas.

His popular radio broadcast *Insight for Living* airs on every major Christian radio market in all fifty states in the U.S., and through more than 2,100 outlets worldwide in numerous foreign languages.

His prolific writing ministry includes more than 70 titles.

www.insight.org

Corrie ten Boom
1892–1983

Corrie ten Boom was a Dutch Christian and Holocaust survivor who helped many Jews escape the Nazis during World War II. Her involvement with the Dutch underground began with her acts of kindness as they gave temporary shelter to Jewish neighbors who were being driven out of their homes. The word spread, and more and more people came to their home for shelter.

The entire ten Boom family became active in the Dutch resistance, risking their lives as they harbored those hunted by the Gestapo. It was estimated that they saved the lives of 800 Jews. All ten Boom family members were incarcerated, including her 84-year-old father, who soon died in prison. Corrie and her sister Betsie were held in the notorious Ravensbrück concentration camp, where her sister died.

Corrie returned to Germany in 1946, then traveled the world speaking in over sixty countries, during which time she wrote several books. She received many tributes, including being knighted by the Queen of the Netherlands.

www.corrietenboom.com

J.C. Ryle
1816-1900

John Charles Ryle was the first Anglican Bishop of Liverpool, England. He was thoroughly evangelical in his doctrine and uncompromising in his principles, a prolific writer, vigorous preacher, and faithful pastor.

He formed a clergy pension fund for his diocese and built over forty churches. Despite criticism, he put raising clergy salaries ahead of building a cathedral for his new diocese. His plain speech and distinctive principles made him a favorite amongst Liverpool's largely working-class population. Ryle combined his commanding presence and vigorous advocacy of his principles with graciousness and warmth in his personal relations. Vast numbers of working men and women attended his special preaching meetings, and many became Christians.

A.W. Tozer

1897-1963

The third of six children raised on a small farm in Western Pennsylvania, Aiden Wilson Tozer was given very little education during his childhood. While on his way home from the Akron, Ohio tire company where he worked as a teen, young Tozer overheard a street preacher say, "If you don't know how to be saved, just call on God." On returning home, Tozer climbed into the attic and followed the preacher's advice.

Many of the more than 40 books Tozer has authored are now considered Christian classics. His writings impress on the reader the necessity to abandon worldly comforts in favor of the deeper life that comes with following Christ.

Kris Vallotton

Kris Vallotton is the Senior Associate Leader of Bethel Church in Redding, California and co-founder of Bethel School of Supernatural Ministry (BSSM). He travels internationally training and equipping people to successfully fulfill their divine purpose. He has a diverse background in business, counseling, consulting, pastoring, and teaching, which gives him unique leadership insights and perspectives.

He is also the founder and president of Moral Revolution, an organization dedicated to global cultural reformation and providing resources that equip and empower society to live in wholeness. Kris is also a bestselling author, having written more than a dozen books and training manuals to help prepare believers for life in God's Kingdom.

www.krisvallotton.com

Rick Warren

Dr. Rick Warren is an American evangelical Christian pastor and author. He founded and is senior pastor of Saddleback Church in Lake Forest, California. He also oversees a global alliance of pastors through the Purpose Driven Network and Pastors.com, an online community that provides sermons and other practical resources for ministers.

Rick is well known for his book *The Purpose Driven Life* which sold over 30 million copies and was a *New York Times* bestseller.

www.PastorRick.com

John Greenleaf Whittier
1807-1892

John Greenleaf Whittier was an American poet and advocate for the abolition of slavery in the United States. He was strongly influenced by the Scottish poet Robert Burns, and was known as one of the "Fireside Poets" or "Schoolroom Poets," a group of popular 19th century American poets.

Although Whittier never stopped writing poetry, his focus changed from the political to pastoral in his later works. He became one of the country's most popular poets.

www.johngreenleafwhittier.com

Philip Yancey

Philip Yancey is an American author who worked as a journalist in Chicago, editing the youth magazine Campus Life, while also writing for a wide variety of other magazines including *Reader's Digest, Saturday Evening Post, National Wildlife* and *Christianity Today*. In 1992, he and his wife, Janet, moved from Chicago to the foothills of Colorado.

Yancey has written a number of books, three of which were coauthored with Dr. Paul Brand, who influenced him more than any other person.

www.philipyancey.com

Ravi Zacharias

Ravi Zacharias is Founder and President of Ravi Zacharias International Ministries (RZIM), a global team of speakers with offices throughout the world. Dr. Zacharias travels extensively and has spoken in over 50 countries and at numerous universities, including Harvard and Princeton. He has authored or edited more than 20 books, and hosts a weekly online radio program, *Let My People Think*, which mixes biblical teaching and Christian apologetics. Dr. Zacharias was born in India but immigrated to Canada with his family.

www.rzim.org/about/ravi-zacharias

About the Author

Three weeks after trusting Jesus as her Savior, Victoria Munro wrote and led her first Bible study. She knew next to nothing about the Bible, but visited the only Bible book store in the city, left with an armload of commentaries and other resources, and went to work. This was definitely a new and mind-stretching challenge, but she had a passion to motivate and inspire others to discover the life-changing treasures God had waiting for them in His Word. She has been writing and leading Bible studies ever since.

Victoria was on the staff of The Navigators, an international, interdenominational Christian organization, for over 12 years in England, the Middle East and the United States. During that time, she grew in her love for and knowledge of the scriptures and of disciple-making. Along with her husband, she also taught small group facilitation skills, which she has shared in seminars and many situations since.

Returning to the U.S. as a widow with two small children, she wrote free-lance articles for Christian publications and was responsible for editing and publishing a weekly newsletter for a large church in Colorado.

Recently, Victoria has written and designed a new series of book and topical Bible studies. These are in-depth, application-oriented studies with additional background commentary. Along with these, she has prepared a group facilitator manual for each that includes small group leaders' questions as well as creative, practical suggestions for each study. Reflecting on these studies, she says, "There is little in life more rewarding than to see someone blossom into the person God designed and destined them to be as they study, allowing the Holy Spirit to transform them through His amazing Word. This is truly my passion!"

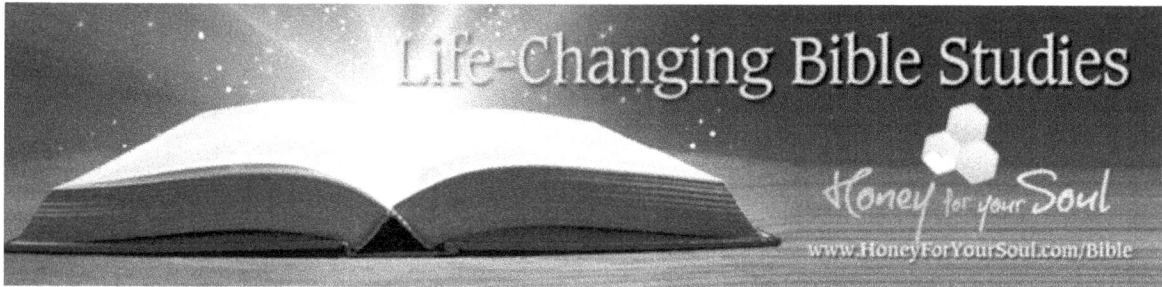
Life-Changing Bible Studies
Honey for your Soul
www.HoneyForYourSoul.com/Bible

Other Bible Studies by Victoria Munro

Explore the Father's Heart: Discover the Depths of His Heart of Love for *You!*

We were created by God for relationship; to be loved and to love. He intended us to be born into families where parents would model His love for their children, but sadly this doesn't always happen. In addition, we live in a fallen world, where children are not always valued and unconditionally loved. As a result, many of us grow up with a distorted view of God.

This study reveals the heart of your good, generous, infinitely patient and always loving heavenly Father. You will get to know, trust and love Him as never before.

The Supernatural Power of Joy: A Study on Philippians

It's easy to regard "joy" as something 'fluffy' – perhaps a bit frivolous. But according to the Bible, nothing could be further from the truth. Joy is a vital aspect of the Christian life!

In this study, you'll look at what joy meant to King David, who certainly experienced the joy of the Lord in challenging situations. You'll also study the book of Philippians and discover how the Apostle Paul drew on the power of joy in very tough times.

Secrets of the Spirit: Jesus' Upper Room Discourse – John 13-17 (Six Studies)

In this series, you'll study Jesus' intimate teaching to His disciples preparing them for a spiritual relationship with Him after He leaves them physically. Within hours of speaking these words, Jesus was hanging on a cross. As you look at His preparation and provision for us in these chapters, you'll better understand the Secrets of the Spirit and how to bear fruit that remains.

Acts of the Spirit: Ordinary People Doing Extraordinary Things (Seven Studies)

This is a practical application-oriented study on the book of Acts. It focuses on how the disciples became effective witnesses in Jerusalem, Judea, Samaria, and throughout the known world; and how He will empower and use us today.

In His Eyes: Studies on the Character of God (Six Studies)

As Christians, there's no study more worthwhile than the attributes of God Himself. We will only entrust our lives to a God we know loves us, is friendly towards us, and wants to meet our deepest needs.

Our goal in this study series is to gaze intently at God, engage with His character, and become more like Him. When you fix your eyes on someone, you not only see that person, you also see yourself reflected in their eyes. By studying the character of God, the source and model of everything you desire to become, you will be changed increasingly into His likeness.

Discussion Group
Leaders' Guide

for

Discover the Royal You!
Training for Reigning

"God means what he says. What he says goes. His powerful Word is sharp
as a surgeon's scalpel, cutting through everything, whether doubt or defense,
laying us open to listen and obey. Nothing and no one is impervious to God's Word.
We can't get away from it—no matter what."
Hebrews 4:11-12 (MSG)

Victoria Munro

Honey for your Soul

Bible Study Series

Discussion Group Leaders' Guide
for
Discover
the
Royal You!
Training for Reigning

Contents

Discussion Group Leaders' Guide
for
Discover
the
Royal You!
Training for Reigning

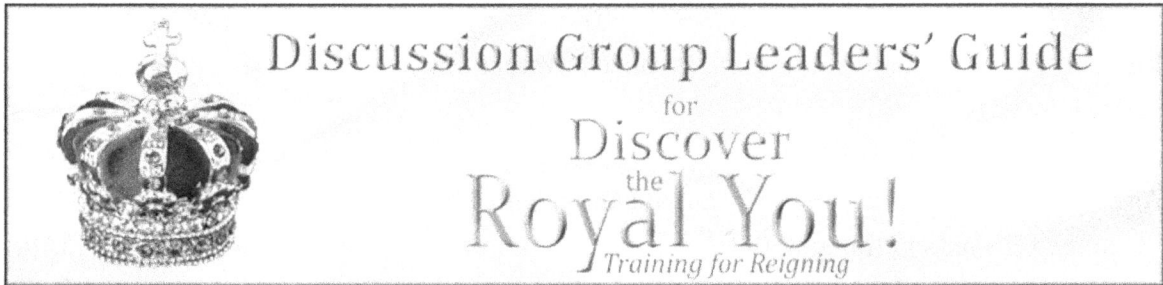

My Experience and Group Discussion Philosophy

Lead a Stimulating Group Discussion

I truly believe that God uses small group Bible study discussions to powerfully transform lives. I've watched Him do it countless times. My goal in this Leaders' Guide is to equip you to facilitate motivating, lively and enjoyable discussions that will result in changed lives.

In addition to my personal philosophy on group discussions, I have included practical facilitator "how-to's" and tips, as well as suggested questions for each study in this series.

I've generally used the word "facilitator" rather than "leader" since this person's goal is not to teach or overtly lead, but rather to guide a stimulating discussion that includes everyone in the group. Effective group facilitating is a different and very rewarding skill that can be easily learned.

❧

My Own Experience

For several decades, I've regularly studied the Bible and it has completely changed my life. However, as a child and young person, I was unaware of the remarkable life-giving power of God's Word.

My parents were not Christians and none of us attended church, but from early childhood something inside me was searching for God. In different ways, I'm sure this is true of everyone. I wanted to know why I was alive and if there truly was a God. If there was,

I wanted to find Him and know Him. I realize now that this was God stirring in me a desire to seek Him.

As a teenager and young person, I was wild and rebellious. I did a lot of crazy things and lived life to the full—or so I thought. But that longing to know God continued to gnaw away inside me. I found my school Bible (in England at that time we were required to have a Bible for school) and began to read it. It made little sense to me. I was a very poor reader and deciphering the Shakespearian English was difficult. Adding to the challenge, I read it late at night and was often too drunk to figure out much of anything. But I continued to read it for years. In my twenties, I even began to visit a local church and attend their weekly Bible study.

I met Jesus at a Billy Graham crusade. When I made the long trek to the front of the auditorium, a lovely woman named Judy stepped out and introduced herself. She talked with me, prayed with me, and then gave a little booklet to me with four Scripture verses printed on cards, assuring me that it would help me if I memorized them.

After that, everything changed. My life was turned upside-down! The Bible changed for me too—it was alive! Overnight this amazing book became God's personal love letter to me, and for the first time, it made sense—well, most of it did. I was hungry and wanted to learn more, much more, and as quickly as possible. This new life was exciting and I didn't want to miss out on any part of it!

The next time I saw my new friend, Judy, she encouraged me to read my Bible each day and ask God to speak to me as I read. She gave me another small booklet titled, *Seven Minutes with God.* "Of course," she explained, "You don't have to just spend seven minutes each day. It would be better to spend more time than that." Since it was summer, I woke up very early in order to read before work each morning. When I met Judy again sometime later, I asked if she thought three hours was enough time to read each day. I wanted to read much more, but I had to work too. I was excited and eager to get to know this God. I wasn't disappointed.

Life was wonderful and everything went smoothly for those first three weeks of my new life. I was learning lots, and receiving excellent teaching with all the encouragement and help I needed. Then one evening my world was shaken. I was completely devastated when the minister leading the weekly Bible studies announced we would stop meeting for three months over the summer. I pleaded with him to continue; told him he simply shouldn't do this to me and the other new believers. It just wasn't right! We needed the Bible study now to learn and grow. But he was adamant about stopping for the summer and suggested that I lead it—me, who knew next to nothing about the Bible!

A few days later, I visited the only Bible bookstore in the city. Climbing the well-worn sandstone steps into a very old, red brick building, I walked into another world—a different era. I felt as though I'd stepped into a Charles Dickens novel. Everything appeared old, dark, and very dusty. It had that musty smell of old books. Two elderly ladies dressed in drab, out-of-style clothes, eyed my mini-skirt disapprovingly, and asked if they could help. They didn't appear to take me seriously or really want to help me. Searching all those shelves loaded with books when I didn't really know what I was looking for was confusing, but I left with an armload of books and commentaries. The weekly Bible study started again the following week.

I hadn't a clue what I was doing, but I learned a whole lot that summer. We studied Paul's letter to the Philippians. I chose it because it was short and seemed relatively uncomplicated. It remains one of my favorite books. People seemed to enjoy the study. God used it to change our lives and I was hooked! I'd witnessed the incredible, life-transforming results and rewards of small group Bible study discussions and was committed to study the Bible and inspire others to do the same as long as I lived!

I encourage you, if you want to know and experience God more intimately and become more like His Son, take time to regularly study His remarkable life-giving Word! Then get involved with others who hunger for more of Him and His Word, and who want to share with each other what He has revealed to them.

〰

Fill your thoughts with my words
Until they penetrate deep into your spirit.
Then as you unwrap my words
They will impart to you true life
And radiant health
Into the very core of your being.
Proverbs 4:21-22 (TPT)

As a non-reader, studying the Bible wasn't and still isn't easy for me, but the rewards have been incredible. I'm not sure I would even have made it through some of life's challenges without the understanding gained through Bible study.

God has put in the heart of each person a longing to know Him. We can try to ignore it and attempt to fill that yearning with all sorts of other things—even really good things. We can look for Him in all the wrong places, as I did for years, but only God Himself can truly satisfy that hunger in our hearts. The Bible leads us to know Him and grow in our friendship with Him. I'm grateful that He gave me a love for His Word. As a new Christian, and still today, I continue to long for more of it. I challenge you to ask God to ignite in your heart a hunger for more of Him through reading, studying, and memorizing this remarkable book, and sharing with others what you have learned.

Why Bible Study?

The gracious hand of his God was on him. This was because Ezra had determined to study and obey the Law of the LORD and to teach those decrees and regulations to the people of Israel. Ezra 7:10

Ezra succeeded at a seemingly impossible task. He recognized his own need and the need of God's people to understand and obey God's Word. Understanding the value and power of His Word, as Ezra did, is an important key to spiritual growth and blessing.

The objective of this study series is to meet and connect with God in His Word and allow the Holy Spirit to change us in that process. These studies are not intended to simply increase readers' knowledge, valuable as that is. Rather the goal is to challenge readers to think deeply, while examining and mulling over truths, allowing the Holy Spirit to speak to their hearts and reveal any changes He would like them to make. Typically there is an application question or two at the end of each study. Since these are important, make sure you leave enough time to cover them in your discussion.

This type of Bible study is time-consuming. It requires serious thought and reflection, but most of all it involves talking with and listening to the Holy Spirit. Jesus promised He would reveal the truth to us.

But when the Father sends the Advocate as my representative—that is, the Holy Spirit—he will teach you everything and will remind you of everything I have told you.
John 14:26

When the Spirit of truth comes, he will guide you into all truth. He will not speak on his own but will tell you what he has heard. He will tell you about the future.
John 16:13

Why Bible Study Discussion Groups?

Loving, supportive and authentic relationships are essential for a healthy, growing church body, as well as for the spiritual growth of all those involved. We were created for relationship with the triune God—Father, Son and Holy Spirit, as well as with one another. We are designed to live in community. Small Bible study discussion groups give opportunity to develop supportive, encouraging and life-giving friendships that are strong and genuine. Establishing a healthy network of relationships like this through small Bible study discussion groups strengthens the church body as a whole, and appears to work well in any culture.

Discover the Royal You! is definitely beneficial for individual study. It was also designed to be used effectively in small group discussions.

The Anatomy of Small Groups

Many different types of groups exist and all have value. The type of discussion group described here can take a little more time and energy to prepare for and facilitate than some others. However, over the years I have found this system produces not only lasting fruit in people's lives, but also deep and continuing relationships. Illustrated below are several types of small groups.

A. **Lecture Style Group**—in this group the leader does all the research, study and preparation; then shares this information with a listening audience.

B. **Lecture Plus Q & A**—the leader here is usually seen very much as the "expert" in the group. This leader teaches and answers questions raised by the participants.

C. **Leaderless Discussion Group**—this type of group can become a bit chaotic. The confident "talkers" tend to dominate, while quiet ones are often left out. Several splinter conversations between members of this group often arise.

D. **Facilitated Discussion Group**—the facilitator is guiding but not teaching or in any way dominating this discussion. She/he makes sure everyone is participating while keeping the conversation on track and on time.

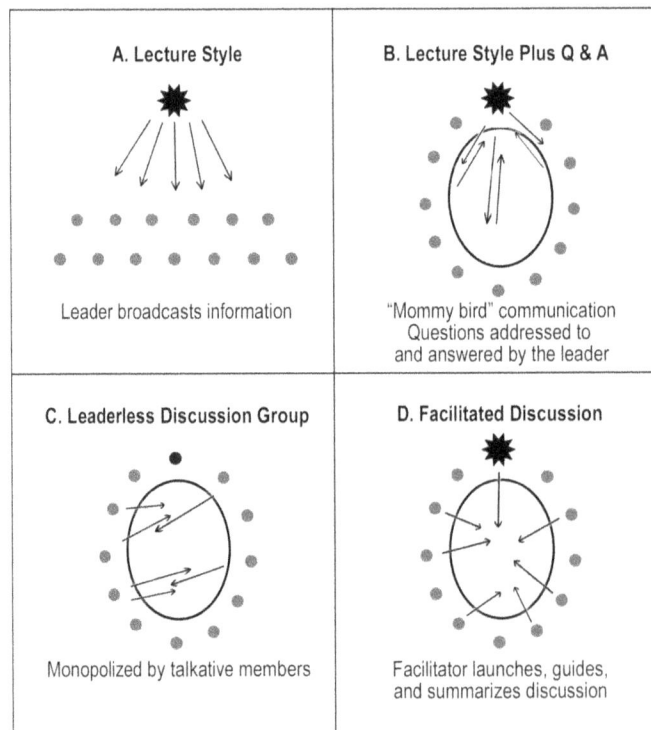

A. Lecture Style — Leader broadcasts information

B. Lecture Style Plus Q & A — "Mommy bird" communication Questions addressed to and answered by the leader

C. Leaderless Discussion Group — Monopolized by talkative members

D. Facilitated Discussion — Facilitator launches, guides, and summarizes discussion

Discussion Group Leaders' Guide

for

Discover

the

Royal You!

Training for Reigning

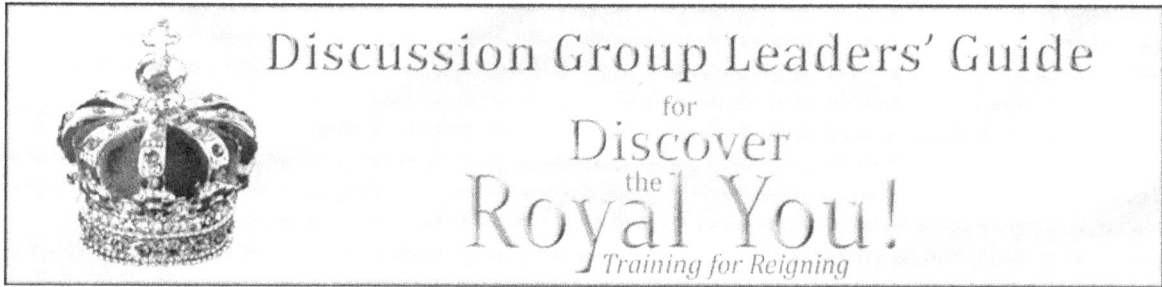

Plan and Prepare

Prepare Yourself

Before starting, you may want to ask God for His vision for your small group Bible studies. Why will they exist? By the end of the series, what would you love to see changed or accomplished? Document this now, so that at the end of the series, you'll have a clear record of all God has done and will be able to thank and praise Him!

Prepare your own heart. Spend time with God. Praise and worship Him. Ask Him to reveal any sin you need to confess and/or anyone you may need to forgive, and fill you with His love. Remember, you don't have to be perfect, just willing to point others to the One who is perfect!

Share your heart with God. Ask Him to help you be genuine and transparent yourself—unafraid to share your own weaknesses and failures as well as strengths and successes. Pray that you will trust and rely on Him more fully. Ask Him to prepare the hearts of each one whom He will bring to the study series, stirring in them an increasing hunger for more of Himself. Be prepared to learn all God has for *you* as you lead this study series.

In these small groups, Jesus *will* be honored and made more real to people; lives *will* be changed; and God's Kingdom *will* be advanced. Because of this, the enemy may be threatened, so don't be surprised if you experience some opposition. Jesus has given you power over him. (See Luke 10:19)

Choose Your Group(s)

Size of Groups – I've found a group size of 8-10 members to be ideal. When leading a larger group, it can be challenging to keep everyone on track, on time and give everyone an opportunity to contribute. If you have fewer members, and a couple of people are unable to attend, it leaves a very small group. However, I've also experienced some of the most powerful and deep discussion times in really small groups.

Type of Groups, i.e. Gender, Age and Spiritual Maturity – Will your group(s) be comprised of women, men, couples, or a mixture? I've found that people share more freely and honestly in groups of the same gender or couples with other couples.

Frequency of Meetings – Will you meet weekly or every other week? Some of these studies are quite long and there is a lot to cover in just one week. Since five of the studies have two sections and one has three, you can easily cover half a study each week. If you choose to meet every other week, I recommend you communicate with group members a few days before to remind them of the next meeting. Also, ask group facilitators to connect with their members via phone, email or even a note in the mail between meetings.

❧

Decide on Your Meeting Agenda

This will depend on your goals for the series. Set times for the following:

Arrival _____

You may want to include a mingle/social time _____

Perhaps a time of worship _____

Group announcements and possibly a brief teaching time _____

Discussion and prayer time _____   Finish Time _____

❧

Create an Ideal Environment

A. The Room

Recent scientific studies reveal that the lighting, temperature, color and sound in a room significantly impact people's mood and productivity. In order to make your study discussion time as meaningful and enjoyable as possible for everyone, paying attention to the atmosphere and making improvements where you can is certainly worth the effort. In light of this, be sure to check out your meeting room well in advance. Ask yourself if it feels warm and inviting. If not, what could you do to make people feel comfortable there?

Is the **lighting** appropriate? If the room feels somewhat institutional with fluorescent lighting, you might try bringing some extra floor lamps. The lighting should enable people to read easily.

How is the **temperature**? Studies show that warmer environments make us happier and more productive, but make sure the room isn't too hot.

Is there **enough space**? If you have several small groups meeting in one room, make sure they can be spaced far enough apart to provide privacy for each group. Some like to lead discussion groups around a table, where they can lay out Bibles and materials, etc. Others prefer groups of chairs in small circles. Both work well. Just remember not to set the chairs in lecture style rows!

Is there a **clock** in the room to keep facilitators aware of the time? They can use their watch or cell phone, but it's much easier to be able to quickly glance up and see the time.

You may also need: a table for registration, name tags, Bible study books, extra pens, and another table for coffee/tea, bottled water and snacks. If you have a large group and will be making announcements or teaching, will you need a microphone? If you have a worship team, what equipment might they need?

B. Welcome

To create a comfortable, easy atmosphere, have worship music playing softly as people arrive. Make guests feel welcome by greeting each one warmly when they arrive; letting them know you're really glad they came. Introduce them to others they may not know.

Help new members to register and make a name badge. Ideally these should simply have their first name in large print. This will help their facilitator and group members learn names and get to know each other more quickly.

Offer them coffee, tea, or bottled water.

It's ideal, especially if the group is large, to have someone else take care of registration and others to greet and answer any questions.

✍

When everyone has arrived and is comfortable, formally welcome them and pray over the time. As you begin, do your best to ensure there won't be any distractions. Ask people to turn off their cell phones.

I like to begin with two or three worship songs.* As well as creating a Christ-centered atmosphere, this helps participants to let go of the cares and worries of their day and focus their attention on Jesus.

*If you don't have a worship leader or aren't musical, talk to your church's worship leader about copyright issues and how you can legally use recorded music.

C. Establish Expectations

Share your goals for the series with everyone, emphasizing the importance of the following:

Confidentiality – What is shared in the group stays in the group.

Preparation – Encourage everyone to come each time with their study completed. Suggest they don't wait until the last minute to prepare their study—it will have less impact, if they finish it in a hurry. It's also much easier to become distracted then. Most people have found answering a few questions each day works best. Explain how the Holy Spirit speaks to everyone differently so each one will come with something of value to share in their group.

Attendance – Emphasize the importance of being at each meeting if at all possible. Each member's contribution is significant, therefore other group members lose out when they're not present.

Be on time – Give them the start and finish times, and share the typical schedule for your meetings.

❧

Plan a Celebration!

At the end of a Bible study series, I usually plan a celebration of some kind—typically a potluck dinner or lunch. It should be a fun and enjoyable time to eat, fellowship, and worship together. After a relaxed time of fellowship and worship, I usually ask some of those who have been involved in the groups to share testimonies of how the series has changed their lives, etc. This can also be an opportunity for participants to invite their friends and learn about the next study series they may want to be a part of.

Discussion Group Leaders' Guide
for
Discover
the
Royal You!
Training for Reigning

Small Group Facilitators

Select, Train and Support First-Rate Facilitators

Over the years, I've learned that excellent small group facilitators don't need to know a great deal about the Bible or to have had experience teaching or facilitating groups. Those who love Jesus, are hungry for more of Him and His Word, and have God's heart of love for people always make the best facilitators!

Meet regularly (at least once a month) with your group facilitators. Get to know them and pray for them daily. Inspire, motivate, challenge, and encourage them.

Explain that as a group leader, they will facilitate a small discussion group and will not be giving a lecture or teaching a class.

Their goal should be to inspire and sustain an absorbing discussion where participants share what they've learned and talk about any questions they may have. The group should be a safe place where people can be real and transparent without fear of judgment.

Set an example yourself by the way you study, how you value and handle God's Word, and how you apply it to your life.

Be honest and vulnerable—share your struggles and concerns—this will create openness and build trust within the group.

Suggest that facilitators prayerfully look for someone who could become their replacement, and mentor that person.

※

Facilitator Preparation Tips

Your purpose as a discussion facilitator is to stimulate group members to think more deeply, share their thoughts and questions, and help them avoid glib phrases, rote answers, and "Christianese." As the facilitator, you're also a cheerleader, friend and guide. You are *not* a lecturer or teacher!

Always arrive early in good time to pray and make any necessary group adjustments, etc.

Start and finish on time. Members need to know when the group will end in order to plan the rest of their day and/or pick up children from childcare.

Pray daily for each of your group members that they will:

- Be faithful to complete their studies.
- Expect to hear from the Holy Spirit.
- Allow Him to work in their lives as they apply what they're learning.
- Attend each meeting.
- Be willing to share what God has shown them.

Ask God to build loving, authentic relationships among group members—that they will support and care for one another. Also ask that your relationships and all you say and do as a facilitator of the group will honor Him.

Remember, as the facilitator, you're the one who sets the tone for the group. Your energy and enthusiasm will be contagious! If you enjoy, laugh and have fun in the group, the others will do the same. If you're loving and caring, they will be too. God has set you with the people in this group, so ask Him to show you how *He* sees them, and give you His heart of love for each one.

Facilitating a group discussion demands concentration. You are constantly scanning group members to see who wants to say something; checking in case anyone is confused; listening to answers and/or comments; guiding the discussion with additional "stirring" questions; keeping everyone on target; and keeping an eye on the time. You are also listening to the Holy Spirit, seeking to understand what He is doing. It is challenging, but so worthwhile and rewarding!

It is really helpful if each group facilitator has an assistant or co-facilitator. This should be someone who will pray with you for the group, be supportive during the discussion times and, if you're unable to attend for any reason, will take over for you.

Discussion Group Leaders' Guide
for
Discover
the
Royal You!
Training for Reigning

Discussion Guidelines

Three Steps to a Stimulating Discussion

Step One – <u>Launch</u>: Throw out a question which is:

Open-ended (cannot be answered with a simple "yes" or "no").

Answerable by anyone in the group.

Relevant to the material group members have studied.

Be comfortable with silence. Having asked your question, wait, looking around the group expecting an answer. ***Don't*** be tempted to break the silence yourself! If you sense group members are confused by the question, you may rephrase it, but don't answer it yourself.

Step Two – <u>Guide</u>: Ask "clarifying" questions, e.g.:

"Tell me what you mean by ____, Jim?"

"Susan, can you expand on that?"

"What makes ____ especially significant to you, Alan?"

"How do you feel about that Sarah?"

"How might you explain that to a non-Christian friend or neighbor?"

Continue to guide and bring everyone into the discussion by interjecting "stirring" questions. For example:

"In what other ways could this text be interpreted?"

"What else might this mean?"

"Can anyone add to that?"

"What does someone else think might be important?"

Step Three – <u>Summarize</u>: Briefly list points made by group members on each section before moving on to the next. If possible, include the names of group members as you sum up what was said.

⤸⤹

During the Discussion

Note: I purposely seldom use the questions already asked in the study itself, but have suggested other questions on the same topics which encourage more thought and discussion.

Listen to the Holy Spirit and stay alert to what you sense He is doing in hearts. Constantly scan the group, paying attention to facial expressions and body language. Remember, only seven percent of our communication is actually with words! Watch for anyone who wants to say something.

Use members' names whenever possible. Honor and affirm each person who contributes; especially when they share something painful or deeply personal. You may want to say something like, "Thank you Jane for sharing that. We really appreciate your honesty and insight."

Make sure you always **explain clearly what you expect** group members to do.

Be a listener—everyone loves to be heard, especially if they're experiencing difficulties.

Sit alert—let your body language communicate that you care and are interested in what they are saying.

Be an encourager—we all need encouragement!

Be comfortable with silence—don't be afraid of it! Some people need time to process and think about what they want to say. It can be tempting to break the silence yourself. *Don't do it!* If you do, you're actually demonstrating to the group that you know more and will answer the questions yourself, so they don't need to say anything. Once you've done this, it's more difficult to get a good discussion started.

⌘

Solutions to Potential Challenges

Deal with the Discussion Dominator: There often seems to be at least one person in a group who has a lot to say and enjoys talking. When someone has been chatting for too long, it's often effective to look away at someone else—we like to have eye contact when we're speaking. If this fails to stop them, I usually wait until they take a breath or interrupt them, graciously thank them for their insights, and turn to look around the group asking what others think about the subject. Tactfully arrange for this person to sit beside you and never opposite you. This seems to help, perhaps because you then have less eye contact.

If you try these ideas and the problem continues, talk with the person one-on-one outside the group setting. I always tell them first how much I appreciate their contributions to the discussions, and then I let them know I really need their help to draw out the quiet ones in the group. This almost always works well.

Draw Out Quiet Ones: I often ask quiet members to read a short scripture. Somehow hearing their own voice seems to build confidence. When you notice someone quiet who wants to speak, look directly at her/him, smile, and using their name, ask what she/he thinks about the subject. Watch for clues that they have something to say. You might encourage them by saying something like, "Just a second, I think Jack wants to add something." When this person does share, affirm and thank them.

However, always **give group members the right** to pass if they don't want to say anything.

Terminate Rabbit Trails: It's important to quickly rein in unrelated tangents. I'm usually quite direct about this, since time is limited and rabbit trails rarely return to the topic at hand. I interrupt and explain that, though this is a fascinating idea, we need to get back on topic in order to get through and finish on time.

Respond to a Wrong Answer: Never tell someone their answer is wrong. Simply ask what anyone else thinks. You may need to ask the questions again.

Resolve Conflicts: Occasionally a conflict may arise in a group. It's a natural consequence of people being together. Don't try to avoid or ignore it, but handle it lovingly. Ask the Holy Spirit to show you what is going on, listen, honor and affirm. Address the issue as He leads you. When handled appropriately, conflicts can create a deeper sense of intimacy within the group. Remember: no judging ever! Always love.

Tend to Your Timing: You will need to pace your discussion to keep on time. On the "Facilitator Questions" sheets in the last section of this book, there is a column on the left in which you can write your times for each study section to help keep you on time. This often works really well, but sometimes the Holy Spirit has other ideas, possibly wanting the group to spend more time on a particular aspect of the study. We want to honor what He is doing. Stop at the designated time, even if you haven't finished the study. Typically I recommend you share prayer requests and pray at the end of the discussion, so be sure to allow time for this.

Since our goal is changed lives, and not simply the acquisition of more knowledge (which of course is of value too), be sure to leave time at the end for group members to share their application questions.

Limit what *You* Share: As a facilitator, you probably know more about the topic being discussed than your group members, but **resist any temptation to teach**. Once you do this, it becomes much more difficult to restart a good discussion. Make it your goal to speak less than anyone else in the group. Share honestly and aim to share only significant gems that could be encouraging to others and are insights they may never have thought of themselves. Sharing valuable nuggets in this way can stimulate others in the group to think more deeply as they study the next chapter.

Avoid Miscommunication by Keeping in Touch: Between meetings, call, email, text or send notes to your group members. If they're involved in social media, you may want to set up a private Facebook page for the group.

Never ever ask a question which can be answered with "yes" or "no." This will instantly kill any discussion.

Never give unsolicited advice.

✑

At least once during the study series, plan a social event just for your group. This could be a dinner or lunch potluck at someone's home, or an evening out together somewhere. This should ideally be a time when you can relax, talk together and deepen relationships.

Some groups have watched movies together, but unless you have the opportunity to discuss what you saw afterwards, this isn't a great time to get to know each other. I suggest you talk about this with your group during the first or second meeting. Decide on what you'd like to do and put a date on the calendar. Otherwise it becomes difficult to fit it into busy schedules.

Both you and your group members can ask new people to join the group.

✑

Group Prayer Time

At the end of each discussion time, I recommend you allow time to share prayer requests and encourage group members to pray for one another during the week. There is a page to record prayer requests at the end of each study chapter. Sharing prayer requests can easily become time-consuming, so remind everyone of the time, asking them to be clear but concise. Asking members to keep requests to themselves and their immediate families will also help.

It's ideal if the group can pray together for requests. Some members may not be comfortable praying aloud in a group yet; so be sensitive to that. I like to change up the prayer time: one meeting we might pray "popcorn" prayers—just one quick sentence prayers (probably lots of them). Another time ask your assistant to start praying and encourage others to join in as

God leads them. You could then pray at the end, making sure all requests are covered. If the time is short, you can break the group into twos or threes to pray for one another.

You may also ask someone to keep a prayer log and record answers to prayer. Briefly review recent answers to prayer each time you meet. This brings glory to God and will encourage everyone in the group.

Review and Learn – Be a Life-long Learner

When everyone leaves, your responsibilities aren't over. While it is still fresh in your mind, review the group experience. What went really well? Who left encouraged? Were there things that you could have done differently or better? As you consider this, be careful *not* to entertain any thoughts of shame or regret, which the enemy might want you to focus on. Your purpose in doing this is simply to keep learning from God so that you can serve Him more effectively.

My Prayer for You

I trust you will grow deeper in your relationship with your heavenly Father, with Jesus and with the Holy Spirit, and that you'll be very much encouraged as you lead others to study and share God's powerful Word. May He richly bless you with His heart of love for those you will serve, lead you clearly, and fill you with His supernatural wisdom. As people learn and talk about the scriptures together, I pray that lives will be radically changed, the name of Jesus will be lifted up and honored and God's Kingdom will be advanced.

Discussion Group Leaders' Guide
for
Discover
the
Royal You!
Training for Reigning

The First Meeting

Get Acquainted

I encourage you to start the initial meeting with some fun ice-breaker questions. This can help members get to know one another in surprising ways.

I've listed some questions below which have worked well in small groups. You may use any of these or make up your own. I suggest you choose several questions, print them, and hand a copy of your list to each group member. Having the questions in their hands gives them time and opportunity to think about what they want to say. Ask someone, ideally your assistant if you have one, to answer one of the questions first, and then move on to the next person. As people feel more comfortable sharing, the time they take to answer tends to get longer. So you may want to set a limit on how long they get to answer.

∽

Suggested Ice-Breaker Questions:

What is the bravest thing you've ever done?

If you could have been at one biblical event, what would it be and why?

What is your favorite Bible verse and why does it have significant meaning to you?

If you could have dinner with any person alive in the world today, who would that be, and what questions would you ask them?

Tell us about a gift you will never forget.

If you could go back in time, who (other than Jesus) would you like to spend a day with?

Besides God, who has influenced you the most in your life?

What is your favorite sound and why?

Discussion Group Leaders' Guide
for
Discover
the
Royal You!
Training for Reigning

Discussion Questions
for Group Facilitators

The following pages are suggested facilitator questions for this Bible study series. These questions are designed for a ninety-minute discussion and prayer time. In order to finish on time, I've not included discussion group questions for every question in the studies. You can write times in the left column that fit your schedule. Being able to see this at a glance as you lead the discussion makes staying on time much easier.

Note: "Clarifying" questions, and in some cases "stirring" questions, are indented to easily differentiate them from the main "launch" questions.

I suggest you adapt these question sheets to fit your group(s) and make a copy for each facilitator.

Study One – The Goodness of God

Facilitator Questions

Before you meet, remember to write the times in the left column for your discussion. Being able to see your ideal times here can help you keep the discussion on time.

Remember to drill down with "guiding" questions, and encourage group members to think more deeply. <u>Don't accept surface answers.</u> Ask, "What do you mean by …?"

Keep the discussion moving with "stirring" questions like, "Can anyone add to that?" Or, "What does anyone else think?"

Time	Questions, etc.
	You likely got to know one another a little at the first meeting, but be sure to welcome anyone who is new to the group this time. Ask everyone to briefly introduce themselves.
	Pray for your time together.
	A. Reflection on the Goodness of God
	Question 1, page 24 What came to mind when you thought about God's goodness? 　What did anyone else think?
	Questions 2-3, pages 24-26 Which verses or aspects of God's goodness impressed you in here? And why? 　Which verse was especially meaningful to someone else? 　What else did God show you about His goodness from these scriptures?

Time	Questions, etc.
	Question 4, pages 26-27 Perhaps ask someone with an unfamiliar translation (The Message, The Passion Translation, etc.) to read Psalm 23. What was especially significant to you here about King David's expression of God's goodness? 　　What else? What did the Holy Spirit show someone else? 　　Can anyone add to that? (Only if you have time): **Questions 6-7, pages 28-30** Which of these passages was most meaningful to you? 　　What did you learn here about God's goodness? **Question 8, page 31** How do you think God's goodness might lead someone to repentance, in a way that punishment or difficulties cannot? **Question 9, page 32** Ask someone to read Psalm 84:11. What does God promise us here? 　　How or in what ways are you sometimes tempted to doubt this promise? 　　What could be a solution to that? ## B. God's Goodness Revealed in Jesus (Only if you have time): **Questions 11-12, page 33** Ask two people to read Matthew 19:16-17 and Luke 12:32 What new aspects of God's goodness do you see here?

Question 13, page 34

Ask someone to read Romans 3:21-26 and Acts 10:38

How did Jesus' actions demonstrate God's goodness in these verses?

Question 14, page 35-36

How does God want us to respond to His goodness?

*Questions 15-16, pages 36-37

Ask the group to share their answers to these questions.

*Application question

Prayer Time:

Ask group members to share prayer requests. Honor privacy by keeping requests to group members themselves and their immediate family.

There is a page to record prayer requests at the end of each study chapter.

Pray – Ask your assistant or someone you know will be comfortable praying aloud to start. Encourage everyone to participate; then close in prayer yourself, making sure all requests are covered.

If you're out of time, ask one of the group members to close in prayer.

Encourage group members to pray for one another. Remind them that many of these requests are **confidential.**

You may want to ask if someone would like to keep a group prayer log or journal and record answers to prayer each time you meet. This can be really encouraging for everyone.

Either you or the person keeping the prayer journal can email requests to everyone, with the subject line: "Confidential Prayer Requests." This helps keep them in touch if anyone is unable to attend a meeting.

End Time.

Study Two – Loved, Chosen and Adopted

Facilitator Questions

Remember to keep the discussion moving with "stirring" questions like, "What else could this mean?" "What does anyone else think?" Or, "Can anyone add to that?"

Time	Questions, etc.
	If you have any new members in your group, welcome them and ask everyone to briefly introduce themselves.
	Ask your assistant to open in prayer.
	A. Loved by God
	Questions 1-2, pages 41-44 How is God's love revealed in the Old Testament? How else? What else did you learn about God's love?
	Questions 3-5, pages 45-47 From these questions, what especially impressed you about God's love for *you*? What was meaningful to anyone else? Can anyone add to that?
	Question 6, page 47 How do we "abide" or "remain" in Jesus' love? (John 15:1-8)
	Question 8, page 48 What did you learn about the Father God's love for you from Jesus' prayer in these verses?
	(Only if you have time): Ask members to share their answers to Question 9, on page 49.

Questions 12-13, page 51

Share your answers to questions 12 and 13.

B. Chosen by God And Adopted into His Family

Questions 14-15, pages 53-56

What did you learn about "being chosen by God" that was new or especially meaningful to you?

> What else? What did anyone else learn?

Question 16, page 57

As a result of being chosen, how should we live differently from those who don't yet know God?

Questions 18-19, page 60

Is anyone willing to share how you see yourself?

> What causes us to see ourselves as we do? What influences you?
> How could we allow God's Word to more effectively influence the way we see ourselves?

Questions 20-22, pages 62-64

From these questions, what did you learn about God's father heart that was most meaningful to you?

> What did someone else learn? What do you mean by …?

*Questions 23-24, page 65

Ask the group to share their answers to these questions.

*Application question

Prayer Time:

Ask group members to share prayer requests and any answers to prayer from the last time. Honor privacy by keeping requests to group members themselves and their immediate family.

Encourage group members to pray for one another. Remind them that many of these requests are **confidential.**

End Time.

Study Three – Reigning in Life

Facilitator Questions

Remember to keep the discussion moving with "stirring" questions like, "What else could this mean?" "What does anyone else think?" Or, "Can anyone add to that?"

Time	Questions, etc.
	If you have any new members in your group, welcome them and ask everyone to briefly introduce themselves.
	Ask one of the group members to open in prayer.
	A. Reigning in Life Every Day
	Ask one of the group members to read the scriptures on page 70.
	What does God promise us in these scriptures? What else?
	Question 2, page 71
	Ask someone to read Ephesians 2:6-7.
	What do you think it means to be seated with Christ now in the heavenly realms?
	How might believing this cause you to change the way you think or act?
	Question 4, page 72
	If you'd been raised in a palace as heir to the throne, how would you see yourself differently than you do now?
	In order to be a successful king/queen, what new thoughts and/or beliefs would you need to adopt?
	Question 5, page 73
	Would anyone would like to share their answer to question 5?

Question 6, page 74

Ask someone to read Philippians 3:20-21

What hope does Paul give his readers regarding their future?

In what ways might this promise be an encouragement to us today?

> What might it mean in practical terms to live as a citizen of heaven on earth?

(Only if you have time):

Question 7, pages 74-75

Which of the scriptures here especially impressed you and why?

B. Truth that Triumphs Over Lies

Questions 8-10, pages 77-79

From questions 8 through 10, what did you learn about the devil and his tactics?

Question 12, page 81

Have someone read 1 Peter 5:8-9.

In light of this truth, what should our response to him be?

Questions 13-14, pages 83-84

Ask someone to read Philippians 4:6-7, John 14:27 and John 16:33.

From these verses, how can we combat fear and anxiety?

Questions 15-16, pages 85-86

What strategies can we use to resist the lie that God doesn't love us?

Questions 17-19, pages 87-89

What did you learn about forgiveness?

What is the biggest challenge you face, or have faced in the past, with forgiveness?

*Question 20, page 90

Is anyone willing to share the lies (that at some level) they are believing or have believed?

*Application question

Optional:

To help everyone remember that these really are **lies** the next time they come to mind, the following little graphic exercise has been helpful to many group members.

The facilitator has a roll of toilet tissue and hands some to each group member. (Note: It's a good idea to check that the kind you bring is easy to write on.) Group members then write on the tissue the lies they've believed. After that, the group goes together to the restroom, one of them prays over the lies, asking God to remind them that these are in fact lies and *not* the truth. Then group members throw their tissue with lies into the toilet and they have a "royal flush!"

Prayer Time:

Ask group members to share prayer requests and any answers to prayer from the previous time. Honor privacy by keeping requests to group members themselves and their immediate family.

Encourage group members to pray for one another. Remind them that many of these requests are **confidential.**

End Time.

Study Four – The Royal Scepter
Your Authority in Christ

Facilitator Questions

Remember to keep the discussion moving with "stirring" questions like, "What else could this mean?" "What does anyone else think?" Or, "Can anyone add to that?"

Time	Questions, etc.
	If you have any new members in your group, welcome them and ask everyone to briefly introduce themselves.
	Ask someone in the group to open in prayer.
	Ask a confident, good reader to read Ephesians 1:17-23, either from page 94 in the book or from their Bible.
	A. Authority Stolen
	Question 1, page 95 What does this passage say about our position in Christ?
	Question 2, page 95 Ask members to share their answers to question 2.
	Question 3, page 96 How do we, or can we, use this power?
	(Only if you have time): **Question 4, page 96** Ask if anyone would like to read what they wrote for question 4.

Questions 5-6, pages 97-98

Ask someone to read Psalms 8:4-6 and 115:16.

To whom did God originally give authority over the earth?

What happened to that authority? What is our position now?

B. Authority Restored

Question 7, page 99

Ask someone to read Colossians 2:11-15.

Exactly what happened to the devil when Jesus died and rose again?

Question 8, page 100

Ask someone to read Matthew 28:18-20.

What do you think it means to "make disciples?"

What else might be included?

C. Exercise Your Authority

Question 10, page 102

Ask someone to read Luke 9:1 and 10:19.

Over what did Jesus give the disciples (and us) authority?

When and how are we to use this authority?

Question 11, page 103

Ask someone to read Mark 4:35-40.

Why do you think Jesus reprimanded the disciples for their lack of faith?

Question 12, page 104

Ask someone to read Matthew 21:18-22.

What did you learn about faith here?

How can we increase our faith?

Question 13, page 104

What might prevent us from using our authority?

Question 15, page 106

From Ephesians 6:12, who are we fighting against?

Who are we *not* fighting against?

Question 17, page 107

Ask someone to read James 4:7 and 1 Peter 5:8-9.

In these scriptures, what are we told to do?

What do you think it means to "resist the devil?"

Question 18, page 109

Where is this battle primarily fought?

What does this look like?

How can we gain victory here?

Question 19, page 110

Ask group members to share their answers to question 19.

Questions 20-21, page 111

What did you learn about our words in this battle?

*Question 22, page 113

Ask group members to share their answers to question 22.

*Application question

Prayer Time:

Ask group members to share prayer requests and answers to prayer from the last time you met. Honor privacy by keeping requests to group members themselves and their immediate family.

Encourage group members to pray for one another. Remind them that many of these requests are **confidential.**

End Time.

Study Five – Royal Relationships

Facilitator Questions

Remember to keep the discussion moving with "stirring" questions like, "What else could this mean?" "What does anyone else think?" Or, "Can anyone add to that?"

Time	Questions, etc.
	If you have any new members in your group, welcome them and ask everyone to briefly introduce themselves.
	Ask your assistant to open in prayer.
	A. Relating to the Godhead – Father, Son and Holy Spirit
	Question 2, page 120 Ask a good reader to read Ephesians 3:14-19, either from page 120 in their book or from their Bible. What does Paul pray for these believers? What does that really mean? 　What might you expect when you pray this way for someone?
	Question 3, pages 120-123 What did you learn about King David's relationship with God from these Psalms? What steps are you taking to apply some of these truths in your life?
	Questions 4-6, pages 123-124 Which of these scriptures especially spoke to you? From what you learned here, how can you strengthen your relationship with God? 　How else? What else could we do?

Question 7, page 125

What was Paul's concern for these believers?

How can we avoid this pitfall ourselves?

Questions 8-10, pages 127-129

From what you learned here, how can you grow deeper in your relationship with God? What do you need to do?

What else? What do you mean by...?

Question 11, page 130

From question 11, what might hinder or prevent our relationship with God from growing deeper?

B. Relating to and Honoring Others

Question 12, page 132

Ask someone to read Matthew 5:43-48.

What did you learn about honor from these verses?

Can you share if there is a person in your life who has not honored you and how you plan to show honor to him or her?

Questions 13-14, pages 133-134

Would anyone like to share when you felt most honored? (least honored?)

Why do you think you find it easy or difficult to receive honor?

Question 15, page 134

Ask a good reader to read John 13:1-17.

What was Jesus teaching His disciples here?

How can we practically apply these lessons in our lives?

Questions 16-17, page 135

Did God show you specific people He would like you to honor? Would you like to share that?

Can anyone share ideas you have for increasing honor at work or home?

Question 18, page 136

What did you learn about honoring and accepting others from these scriptures?

Question 19, page 136

Ask someone to read Colossians 3:12-14.

How do we "put on" love? What do you think this means?

Question 20, page 137

Ask someone to read Philippians 2:1-11.

What did Paul tell his readers would make him truly happy?

How might Jesus' example here motivate you to honor others?

Question 21, page 138

How are we to honor those who don't yet know Jesus?

What is our role? In what ways can we show them His love?

*Question 22, page 139

Ask if anyone would like to share about how they plan to honor and show God's love to those on their list.

*Application question

Prayer Time:

Ask group members to share prayer requests and answers to prayer. Keep requests to group members themselves and their immediate family.

Encourage group members to pray for one another. Remind them that many of these requests are **confidential.**

End Time.

Study Six – Pursue Your Divine Destiny

Facilitator Questions

Remember to keep the discussion moving with "stirring" questions like, "What else could this mean?" "What does anyone else think?" Or, "Can anyone add to that?"

Time	Questions, etc.
	If you have any new members in your group, welcome them and ask everyone to briefly introduce themselves.
	Ask a member of the group to open in prayer.
	A. Discover Your Destiny
	Question 1, pages 143-144 What did you discover about God's will from the scriptures on pages 143 and 144? What else? Ask anyone to read verses that were especially meaningful to them.
	Question 2, page 145 Ask if anyone would like to share their answers to question 2.
	Question 3, page 146 How do you think we can apply Jeremiah 29:11-13 to our lives today? What condition does God make here? What could prevent this?
	Question 4, page 147 Who would like to share their answers to question 4?

Question 5, pages 147-150

From the passages on pages 147 to 150, what can we do to be sure that God is guiding us in *His* ways?

How can we hear His voice more clearly?

Question 6, pages 150-151

What answers did anyone have for question 6?

How can we benefit by having advisors in our lives? How else?

Question 7, pages 151-152

What spiritual gifts do you feel God has given you?

How do you want God to use these in the future?

What are you doing now to prepare for that?

Question 8, page 152

Would anyone like to share words they've received that relate to their destiny?

Questions 9-11, pages 153-154

What did you learn about yourself from your answers here?

What else? What did anyone else learn?

How might this affect your future?

Question 12, page 155

What answers did you have for question 12?

Question 13, page 155

Ask someone to read Psalm 105:15-23.

What did you learn from Joseph's example? What else?

How might this help or encourage you?

B. Overcome Obstacles Along the Way

Questions 14-16, pages 157-158

When facing a seemingly insurmountable problem what can we do?

How do we do this?

Would anyone like to share their answers to questions 14, 15 or 16?

Question 17, page 158

What can we do to remain focused on our God-given destiny?

What else might we do?

Question 18, pages 159-161

Ask several different people to read John 13:37-38, Matthew 26:69-75, Mark 16:7, John 21:17 and Acts 2:40-41.

How did Peter deal with regret?

How did Jesus encourage him? What was the result?

What can we learn from his experience?

Question 19, pages 161-162

Ask someone to read Philippians 3:13-14.

How did Paul handle regret?

(Only if you have time):

Question 20, page 162

How can Romans 8:1 encourage us when we're tempted to focus on past failures and/or mistakes?

*Question 21, page 163

Ask everyone to share their answers to question 21.

Encourage anyone who hasn't completed this question to do this later.

*Application question

Prayer Time:

Ask group members to share prayer requests and answers to prayer.

If you have an end of the series celebration, remind them of the day and time, what they should bring, etc.

End Time.

www.ingramcontent.com/pod-product-compliance
Lightning Source LLC
Chambersburg PA
CBHW050714100426
42735CB00042B/3352